The Greatest Guide to

This is a **GREATEST**GUIDES title

Greatest Guides Limited, Woodstock, Bridge End, Warwick CV34 6PD, United Kingdom

www.greatestguides.com

Series created by Harshad Kotecha

Greatest Guides is committed to a sustainable future for our planet. This book is printed on paper certified by the Forest Stewardship Council.

MIX
Paper
FSC   FSC® C020837

Printed and bound in the United Kingdom

ISBN 978-1-907906-01-5

I would like to dedicate this book to:

My dad, Philip; my mum, Sylvia
My wife, Karen; and my sons, Mat & Ben

They truly are a great family.
A big thank you!

Gary Player and family
Apart from my immediate family, Gary and his family have been the biggest influence in my professional golfing career. Gary, you treated me like a brother, I hasten to add, much younger brother! Your help and guidance, the hours and hours we spent working on our golf swings has helped me to become hopefully one of the best golf teachers in the world.

I do not believe I ever go through a day of coaching without bringing your name up. Thank you for being my friend.

Butch, Dick, Bill and Craig Harmon
Without doubt, the best golfing family in the world! Their father, Claude, won the Masters in 1948 and a great deal of the golfing knowledge and experience they have, comes straight from him. I have only known you all for a few years but the time we have spent together, coaching the juniors from Great Britain and Ireland has been tremendous fun.

You are the greatest golf teachers in the world, it is an honour to know you.

Contents

Foreword by Gary Player ...

I have known John for over 30 years. I consider him to be a close friend, and a wonderful teacher of the game of golf – certainly one of the very finest short game coaches teaching players today.

Our friendship, and the adventures we shared during the long hot summers John stayed with me on my farm in South Africa, when I was the number one golfer in the world and he was a fresh faced young pro bursting with confidence on the back of winning the English Amateur Championship and British Youths Championship, can be seen as an example of the good things and opportunities that this game can give us. I have been lucky enough to travel the world many times over, and to meet people from all walks of life, through golf. In an age when ethics and values are constantly undermined, this sport truly brings out the best in people, by encompassing the virtues of honour, respect, hard work and personal achievement – all of which matter more than ever in today's modern world!

John and I share many of the same ideas about playing the game. He possesses a wonderful, intuitive gift for imparting his knowledge and technical instruction both simply and effectively. He is a teacher with both humor and empathy, and is a man who is respected throughout the golfing community. The tips and advice in this book will help your golf game immensely, and, I hope, will bring you many hours of fun on the course. You can use the book time

and time again for reference, and I hope you have as much
enjoyment reading these amusing and informative pearls of
wisdom on the game as I have.

Best wishes

Gary Player

Teeing off
& Driving

" "After all, golf is only a game," said Millicent. Women say these things without thinking. It does not mean that there is a kink in their character. They simply don't realize what they are saying. "

P G Wodehouse, Order by Golf

Chapter 1

Teeing off & Driving

Any more than fourteen clubs in your bag will incur penalty shots, so, before you tee off on the first hole, check that you only have fourteen, and check that you have a score card, a pencil, enough balls to last the round, tees, a towel if it looks like rain, an umbrella, and an energy drink. You are probably going to spend the best part of four hours on the course, so don't get caught out.

QUICK T!P

ASSERT YOURSELF TO GAIN ADVANTAGE IN MATCH PLAY
You can get off to a great start in match play by asserting yourself on the first tee. As soon as you meet your opponent on the tee, tell him the number of the ball you are using; if he was going to use the same number, he'll be forced to change his ball. This may be your opponent's lucky number ball, which he has to change because you asserted yourself!

Hit the tee from under the ball

A great tip, to keep you down through your drive swing, is to try and hit the tee out from under the ball. If you are inclined to top the occasional drive, this will be the answer to your prayers.

Tee ball high to hit it low

When you are driving into the wind, the last thing you want is for the ball to go too high. You would think that the obvious thing to do, when trying to hit the ball low with your driver, is to tee it low. When the ball is teed low it encourages a steeper approach into the ball, often resulting in too much backspin; the head wind gets under it, causing the ball to fly high with no penetration.

Next time you want to hit the ball low into the wind with your driver, try teeing the ball a little higher than you would for your normal drive. Then hit the ball clean off the top of the tee, without making contact with the tee. You will find the ball flies lower with much more penetration.

How to drive the ball consistently

'Drive for show – putt for dough' is a famous saying. Well, if you do not drive the ball onto the fairway, you will not have many putts for dough. You will have plenty of putts to save, losing more dough. We seem to have a mental thing about needing to hit the ball harder with our driver than we do with any other club. A wild slash at the ball, and so on.

The best tip I have heard, relating to consistency with the driver, is to try and make the best and most balanced swing you have ever made. This thought in your mind will encourage you to swing with more rhythm; it will also stop any kind of a slash at the ball. Try it this weekend, it will work.

How to drive the ball further

As a golf coach, the most common question I get asked is 'how do I hit the ball further with my driver'? Well, it is not by having a wild swipe at the ball, as I explained in my previous tip. There are a few ingredients required, you can add one at a time, and then see the increased distance you hit the ball with your driver…

1. Stand with your feet the width of your shoulders.

2. Stand tall, this will help you create width in your swing.

3. Make a complete 90 degree shoulder turn during your backswing. This is when your left shoulder points at the ball.

4. At the top of your backswing, the knuckle on the thumb of your right hand should be well away from your right shoulder. This will create a wide arc.

5. Start the downswing with an uncoiling motion from your left hip. At the same time, keep the width in your arms (a wide gap from the knuckle on your right thumb and your right shoulder). This will give you leverage.

6. Do not be frightened to release the club head through impact. This creates club head speed.

7. Turn right through, onto your left foot; your belt buckle should now be facing the target.

8. Hold onto a balanced follow through.

9. Maintain your height throughout the swing.

You cannot possibly think of all these things in one swing, so perfect one move at a time, and hit that ball further.

Mark your ball

You may have seen the Tour Professionals mark their ball with a permanent marker, some put dots above or below the number, some will put on their initials, some draw a smiley face, etc. You may wonder why they do that, when they would check that they were playing with a different number ball than their opponent's. Here is the reason…

If, when reaching your ball, you found another ball of the same make, with the same number, lying nearby, one that had been hit by a player not in your match, both balls would be deemed lost if you were unable to identify your ball. A two stroke penalty!

The same could happen if your ball ended up in the rough, near a similar ball that had been lost earlier, making it impossible for you to identify

Player Profile   JACK NICKLAUS

Height:	5' 10"
Born:	January 21st 1940
Birthplace:	Columbus, Ohio, USA
Turned Pro:	1961

Jack Nicklaus won 73 PGA Tour events in his career. With 18 Majors Championship titles, 19 second places, and 9 third places, it is a record some say may never be beaten. In all, he posted 48 Top 3 finishes, 56 Top 5 finishes, and 73 Top 10 finishes. Jack Nicklaus represents the very essence of sporting achievement, and is arguably the greatest golfer ever.

Nicklaus brought power to the forefront in golf, being the longest driver of his generation. But he was also one of the best clutch putters ever, and his concentration skills were legendary. Jack is also credited as being one of the pioneers of the sport, having helped turn golf into the major spectator sport it is today.

In addition, Jack claimed over 100 tournament titles between 1962, when he joined the professional ranks, and in 2005, when he bowed out memorably, at The Open Championship at St. Andrews. As a tribute to his achievements, in the same year, Royal Bank of Scotland used Jack's image on a special issue of two million commemorative £5 notes.

His retirement from the sport has allowed Jack to further develop his extensive interests off the course, which includes his golf course design, equipment, and clothing businesses.

Jack was inducted into the World Golf Hall of Fame in 1974.

which ball is yours. Same penalty! Get into the habit of putting your mark on the ball, and save those unnecessary penalties.

Ball position

To hit the ball the maximum distance when driving, the ball must be struck at the bottom of the arc, or slightly on the upswing. It must not be struck during the downswing. The position of the ball at address will determine how the ball is struck. If the ball is too far back, you will strike it too early in your turn, making the ball go right. If the ball is too far forward, you will strike it too late in your turn, making the ball go left. I have always found that if the ball is opposite the instep of my left foot it is about right.

The Clouds are your friends

Many teeing areas are sheltered by trees or hedges, sometimes to the extent that you do not feel the wind blowing from any particular direction. As soon as your tee shot gets above the trees, the wind blows the ball off line.

Remember, the clouds are your friends and they are telling you the direction the wind is blowing, so, before taking your shot, always make sure you check with your friends and allow for the information they give you.

The Swing

" The golf swing is like a suitcase into which we are trying to pack one too many things. "

John Updike

Chapter 2
The Swing

If you grip the club with an unorthodox grip, you have to swing with an unorthodox swing to compensate. The best way to put your hands on the club is to feel like you are shaking hands with the club with your left hand. You should be able to look down at your hand and see two to two and a half knuckles. The right hand joins in such a way that your right and left hands are parallel to one another. The grip should now be held with the upper part of the fingers of the right hand. You can either have all your fingers of both hands on the grip, this is called the two-handed grip, or overlap the index finger of your left hand with the small finger of your right, called the Harry Vardon grip. The other grip is when you interlock the index finger of the left hand with the little finger of the right. Try each grip to find out which one works best for you.

Stand as though you are about to save a penalty

The easiest way I have found to explain the correct set up position is to imagine yourself in goal, standing as though you are about to save a penalty. You will notice that your feet are about the width of your shoulders, your knees are flexed, and you are bending slightly, from the waist. You are now ready to put the club down behind the ball and fire.

66 Golfers, when in a temper, throw their clubs backwards, and that's wrong. You should always throw a club ahead of you so that you don't have to walk any extra distance to get it! 99

Tommy Bolt

Turn your right foot out to help you turn

If you struggle to complete your backswing, you will surely be losing distance. This happens to us less supple people, who have put on a pound or two around the waist.

The easy cure is to turn your right foot out a little at address, this will allow your hips to turn easier during the backswing. The less supple you are, the more you need to splay your right foot.

QUICK T!P
HOLD YOUR CHIN HIGH TO MAINTAIN POSTURE
As I have mentioned earlier, you must stay tall throughout the swing; you need something simple in your mind to make that happen. Think of your chin, keep your chin high throughout the swing. It is much easier to think of your chin than of your entire body.

Are you hooking the ball?

There are a few reasons why you could be hooking, though one thing is for sure, you are striking the ball with the club face closed. This will impart anti-clockwise spin, making the ball hook. The first thing you must check is that, at the top of your backswing, the thumb on your left hand is directly under the shaft; if it is not quite under, you will be closing the club face during the backswing. This will be the cause of your hook.

Are you slicing the ball?

Whether your ball is starting left of the target and then slicing, or starting at the target and slicing, it means that you are striking the ball with the club face open. This is often caused by a reluctance to release the club head with your right hand. When you next go to the practice ground, hit balls only with your right hand, get used to the feeling of your right hand striking the ball. This will square the club face at impact and help to cure that slice.

Are you topping the ball?

When I learnt how to play golf, I was told, as I am sure many of you were, that, if I topped the ball, it was because I had lifted my head. What rubbish! The main reason for topping the ball is because you straighten your legs during your swing, this raises your body, resulting in a topped shot. Ensure you keep your knees flexed during your swing, as they were at address.

QUICK T!P
IS THE PROBLEM A HEAVY SHOT?
Are you taking a deep divot when playing your shots? Find a place on the practice ground where you can hit balls that are above your feet. This will give you a swing plane that is not so steep and eliminate those heavy shots.

Stopping the flat backswing

If the club is taken back on a flat plane, it is getting too far behind your body, and too low. This will cause the club to get trapped behind you during the downswing. Block shots to the right, and snap hooks, are the normal result. A great tip is to get an old club and stand with your back against a wall, so that your heels are about six inches away from the wall. Swing the club back, without touching the wall, and you will soon train yourself to swing the club on a better swing plane.

QUICK T!P
BALL STARTING LEFT OF TARGET?
When the ball keeps starting left of the target, and you are not getting a good solid strike on it, this means you are coming over the top of the ball; the club is coming down on an outside to inside direction. The quick way to stop this happening is to start the downswing, letting your left shoulder separate away from your chin. This will automatically slot the club into the correct position for a solid hit.

Player Profile — LEE TREVINO

Height:	5' 7"
Born:	December 1st 1939
Birthplace:	Dallas, Texas, USA
Turned Pro:	1960

Lee Trevino's is a classic story of poor boy made good. Brought up near the United States/Mexico border, this 'Texican' learned his golf with a bottle in hand – to hit the ball with, not to drink from. He developed what was termed an 'agricultural' swing, but, whatever it looked like, then and now, it has earned Trevino a fortune. He is a magical shot-maker, and he has a fast wit, which he has used to entertained crowds all over the globe.

Trevino's first significant victory could have hardly been more auspicious – the 1968 US Open. Three years later, he collected the 'Triple Crown' – the US, Canadian, and British Opens – within 20 days. He retained his Open title the following summer. Since then, Trevino has twice won the US PGA Championship, in 1974 and 1984, but the Masters will now surely elude him.

It has been suggested that Trevino's magnificent career would have been still more glittering, had he not been struck by lightning during a tournament in Chicago in 1975, an incident that has caused him recurring, and severe, back problems. On the US Senior tour (what he calls the 'fat-bellies circuit'!), Trevino has won 16 times.

Player Profile BEN HOGAN

Height:	5' 7"
Born:	August 13th 1912
Died:	July 25th 1997
Birthplace:	Stephenville, Texas, USA
Turned Pro:	1929

There is, and always will be, a certain mystique about the quiet, and focused, Ben Hogan. Those fortunate enough to watch him play say he was the greatest ball striker of all time.

Hogan's first PGA Tour event was the 1932 Los Angeles Open. He finished 38th, to win $8.50. Hogan won 30 tournaments before winning his first major (1946 PGA Championship). That's the record for most wins prior to a first major.

In 292 career PGA Tour events, Ben Hogan finished in the top 3 in 47.6% of them. He finished in the top 10 in 241 of those 292 events. Hogan turned pro in 1929, at age 17, but he didn't join the PGA Tour until 1932. For much of his early career, Hogan battled a hook. In 1940, he began winning, often.

From August 1945 to February 1949, Hogan won 37 times. From 1950 onwards (following a bad car crash in 1949), he never played more than 7 PGA Tour events in a year, yet he won 13 more times, including 6 majors. Until Tiger Woods did it in 2000, Hogan was the only man to win three professional majors in one season. That was in 1953, when Hogan won the Masters, U.S. Open, and British Open.

Ben was inducted into the World Golf Hall of Fame in 1974.

Drop a plumb line down from your right shoulder

If you have been told that you do not get your weight across to your left foot, and you find it just about impossible to do so, try this. Start the downswing with an uncoiling movement from your left hip, then make sure that your right shoulder drives on through. If you have done it properly, you should be able to drop a plumb line from your right shoulder and find that it lands in front of where the ball was at address. If your right shoulder finishes behind the original ball position, it is impossible to get your weight across to the left side.

Look at your grip if the ball ends up slicing

When the ball starts towards the target, the swing plane is correct. If the ball then turns from left to right, the club face is open at impact. Nine times out of ten, it is because of the grip. If this is happening to your shots, turn both hands clockwise round the grip, about a 1/2 inch. Commit to hitting the ball with the new grip, even if it feels very awkward at first.

Firm grip on the backswing

Letting go of the club with your left hand at the top of the backswing is a common fault. It can cause you to start the downswing with a re-gripping of the club, a casting action follows. I believe that the best grip to use is the interlocking grip, where the index finger of your left hand and the little finger of your right hand interlock. I am sure this will help you hold onto the club at the top.

Incidentally, Jack Nicklaus, Greg Norman, and Tiger Woods have all become the best players in the world using the interlocking grip.

An easy cure for that shank

The shank is a shot that can very easily make you give up the game, it can be like a disease you cannot get rid of. There are a number of reasons why a player shanks the ball, but they all have one thing in common. By the time you have taken the club back, and then returned it to the ball, the club head has got further away from you, resulting in the ball being struck in the shank of the club. The cure is the opposite of what you would expect. I would like you to address the ball opposite the shank, and try to hit the ball off the toe of the club. This will reverse your error and stop your shank immediately.

Look high to hit high, look low to hit low

Quite often, it is not advisable to change your swing to deliberately hit the ball high or low.

The best way is to address the ball and look high, for the shot you want to fly high. You will notice that you will naturally put the ball a little forward in your stance, your weight will favour your back foot, and you will picture a full follow through, all things necessary to hit the ball high. When trying to hit the ball low, look low. The ball will be addressed slightly back in your stance, your weight will favour your front foot, and you will naturally shorten your follow through.

QUICK T!P

IMPROVE YOUR RHYTHM WITH ERNIE

Even if you have a technically correct golf swing, you will hit bad shots if your rhythm is not good. You can look at this another way, even if you do not have a technically correct golf swing, you will hit many fine shots if your rhythm is good. I would recommend that you do as the best players do, either count one during the backswing and two during the downswing and follow through, or, say, Ernie during the backswing and Els during the downswing and follow through. Don't say it out loud, otherwise people will wonder about you!

> **" If you drink, don't drive. Don't even putt. "**

Dean Martin

Stop slicing & hit the ball further

The reason a sliced ball does not go as far as a draw is because the right hand does not release the club head through impact. Gripping the club too tightly with your left hand makes it impossible to create a good release.

Next time you go out for a few holes, grip very lightly with your left hand, right through impact, your right hand will now take over, resulting in a square club face, and a much faster club head speed.

Are you getting caught up?

The ball has landed under a tree, wrecking any chance of making a normal swing. It can result in an embarrassing air shot, or a thud as your club embeds itself into the top of the ball. Set the club, look at the ball... and hit. If your club keeps getting caught up in the branches at the top of the backswing, then try setting your club at the top of the backswing, well away from trouble. Leave the club where it is, look down without moving your body, and focus on the ball. Now hit it. Just swing the club down and through the ball.

Shaping the shot – left to right

I bet there are a great number of you who can already shape the shot from left to right without trying, only trouble is, the ball does not end up where you want it.

There are a few ways to make the ball move one way or another in the air, but the art is to land the ball on the spot you were aiming at. The best way to hit the ball with a controlled left to right spin is as follows:

1. Aim your feet, hips, and shoulders in the direction you want the ball to start.

2. Open the club face, until it points at the spot where you would like the ball to land. Then grip, do not grip before you open the club face.

3. Swing the club as you would normally, along the direction of your body. This will start the ball left of your obstacle.

4. Commit to striking the ball with the open club face.

The ball will come off the club with clockwise spin, turning the ball the required amount.

Shaping the shot – right to left

To hit the ball from right to left, take the opposite action to the previous tip.

1. Aim your feet, hips, and shoulders in the direction you would like the ball to start.

2. Close the club face, until it points at the spot you would like the ball to land, then grip. Do not grip before you close the club face.

3. Swing the club as you would normally, along the direction of your body. This will start the ball right of the obstacle.

4. Commit to striking the ball with a closed club face.

The ball will come off the club with anti-clockwise spin, turning the ball the required amount.

The punch shot

The punch shot can be very useful when you are playing on links courses, shots against the wind, or even cross wind, when they are best kept low. The shot is normally played with either a medium iron or a short iron, although there are players who use it with their longer clubs as well. When Tiger Woods plays his low drilling shot with a long iron or three wood, which he calls his stinger, it is played the same way as a punch shot.

When playing the punch, hold low down the grip, put the ball back in your stance, swing the club back to a position half way between your waist and

Player Profile BYRON NELSON

Height:	6' 1"
Born:	February 4th 1912
Died:	September 26th 2006
Birthplace:	Long Branch, Texas, USA
Turned Pro:	1932

Just as there is no argument that perfection in golf is unattainable, no one argues that Byron Nelson came the closest to attaining it.

In a relatively brief career, Nelson won 54 sanctioned tournaments, including the Masters in 1937 and 1942, the U.S. Open in 1939, and the PGA Championship in 1940 and 1945. In the '40s, he finished in the money 113 consecutive times. Nelson reached his peak as World War II was ending, and retired from full-time competition after that 1946 season, but his streak of 11 victories in a row in 1945 is considered the least attainable record, not only in golf, but in sports. His total that year, of 18 victories, 7 second-places, 19 consecutive rounds under 70, and a scoring average of 68.33, set the standard for the greatest, single season in the history of the game.

Tall and rangy, at 6' 1", with enormous hands, Nelson developed an action that is considered to be the basis for the modern golf swing. Coming of age just as the steel shaft was replacing hickory, Nelson learned that using the big muscles in the hips and legs could be a more reliable, powerful, and effective way to hit a golf ball than the more wristy method that had been employed in the era of hickory.

shoulders, follow through just to waist height. The ball will go much lower, and with fizz.

Your distance from the ball at address

In order to strike the ball consistently from the middle of the club face, it is important to stand the correct distance from the ball. Here is an easy way to remember: when you have set up to the ball with an iron, drop the club grip down onto your left leg, with the top of the grip four inches above your knee. When you are setting up to use a wood, drop the club grip onto your left leg, with the top of the grip four inches above your knee.

Wide swings hit the ball further

I have never seen anyone with a narrow swing hit the ball very far.

The next time you see a long hitter, take note of how they take the club back on a very wide arc. The easiest way I have come across to do this is to make sure that, at the end of the backswing, the gap between the knuckle on your right thumb and your right shoulder is as wide as possible. From a wide backswing you can create far more leverage during the down swing – a definite power source.

Don't hit harder, hit better

It always seems amazing how far some players hit the ball, even though they look as though a good wind would blow them over.

Anthony Kim & Rory McIlroy are two great examples, so how do they do it?

Neither of them try to over power the ball, they both try to strike the ball better, with oodles of clubhead speed. You will also notice how balanced they both are at the completion of their swings. This is not something that happens to the players who try to hit the ball with brute force.

Draw a wheel

If you could imagine you had a pencil on the end of the clubhead – your swing should draw a perfect wheel resting on your shoulders, this is the perfect swing plane.

As you take the club back, turn your right hip at exactly the same time as your hands start to move, this will give you a perfect wheel. If your hands go first and then, a little after, your right hip starts to turn, you will create a buckle in the wheel, resulting in inconsistent shots.

Repetition is the answer

Everyone has a different looking swing.

I can recognize a player 250 yards away by looking at their swing.

A lot of the time, we try too many things in our swings, trying to get the perfect technique. The best advice I can give is to work on two or three movements that work for you, keep working on those movements only and perfect your technique.

Repeating the same swing time and time again is what the best players do – none of them look the same, so it proves there is not only one swing to suit all.

Do you think you would be a better player if, over a period of time, you hit 5,000 balls just working on the two or three movements that work for you, or if you hit 5,000 balls while trying lots of different movements. One way helps you perfect your technique, the other way gets you confused.

Is there a swing secret?

When I played on the European and African Tours, I used to think there must be a secret to the swing and that nobody had told me yet, so I made a point of asking as many of the top players as I could.

When I look back, although I did not realize it at the time, they all told me the same thing. They all told me the most simple of things, they were all working on simple basics and, if anything went wrong, they just checked the two or three things that they knew worked for them. One of these players was the British Professional, Tommy Horton. I used to play quite regularly with Tommy and, when we both came off the tour, we lost contact for many years. I was then asked to open a golf course in Essex and play alongside Tommy, during the round I asked him what he was working on in his swing, he told me and I quickly realized they were the same things he had told me about all those years before – Tommy was a great player.

I remember being at the Gary Player Country Club in South Africa, the event was the Sun City Classic – I watched Bob Charles, the famous Left Handed player from New Zealand, he had a long chip shot on the 71st hole, where he had to negotiate quite a few contours on the green. He played the most fantastic shot and very nearly holed it. After the round, I asked him what his thoughts were when he was playing the shot, I expected him to tell me about the technique he used to play the shot, he didn't, he just said he was trying to hole it!

Old or New?

Having taught golf for many years, I have seen many changes in the way players swing the club and play the game.

Many years ago, golf was played by judging the distance, deciding what type of shot you wanted to play – high, low, fade or draw – and then selecting a club that would produce the required shot. Next, players or their caddies would pace the course out and put all the information on a pad, to refer to during their round, distance from the back of a bunker to the pin for example. The next thing we saw were yardage books purchased in the professionals shop, these had diagrams of the holes with yardages from various key points. Now the latest gives us measuring devices that are very accurate and let the player know exactly how far they have to hit their shot.

Iron Play & Fairway Woods

" The number of shots taken by an opponent who is out of sight is equal to the square root of the sum of the number of curses heard plus the number of swishes. "

Michael Green

Chapter 3
Iron Play & Fairway Woods

Put yourself in a position where you have hit a super drive, only to find that the ball has come to rest in an old divot – you think you are the unluckiest player in the tournament. The ball must be struck on the downswing, squeezing the ball out from the bad lie. 'Easier said than done', I can hear you saying. A great tip is to look at the front of the ball throughout the address and downswing; this will make you hit the ball first, then the turf. If it is a short iron you are playing, allow for plenty of backspin.

QUICK T!P
LONG IRONS
I am sure that it is widely recognized that long irons are the hardest clubs to use. Do not fret, help has arrived in the form of a rescue club. It looks half iron, half wood, and makes it easier to play shots of the distance you would normally use a long iron for. I am sure it is the best introduction to a set of clubs for a very long time. If you have not got one, get one! The club is far more forgiving than the 3 or 4 irons, getting the ball into the air much quicker, but still hitting the ball distances you would expect a good long iron to travel.

Long iron or fairway wood?

There is only one reason to use a long iron, as opposed to a fairway wood, and that is when you are playing on a links course, trying to keep the ball low, allowing it to run onto the green. Many links courses were designed for this type of shot, and do not have bunkers guarding the front of the greens.

" Columbus went around the world in 1492. That isn't a lot of strokes when you consider the course. "

Lee Trevino

Know your mid-iron distances

Accuracy is very important. We tend to forget that accuracy includes distance as well as direction, so it is important to know how far you hit each of your mid irons. The 5 iron through to the 7 iron are what we normally regard as mid irons. Of course, it's not much help to know how far each club goes without knowing exactly how long a shot you have to play, so always have a yardage chart handy. To know how far you have to go, and to know how far each club goes, will give you loads of confidence to play the shot well.

The best players are always balanced when they play this shot, they never seem to be hurried, and they never try to hit the ball too hard.

Mid iron v. the wind

When playing a mid iron to the green, always have one rule that you never break. If you are caught between two clubs into the wind, always hit the ball softer with the straighter faced club. Down wind, always hit harder with the more lofted club. If you do it the other way round, you will get too much elevation against the wind, and you will quit on the shot down wind.

Short iron technique

Always picture the ball fading in towards the hole, this will help you put the correct spin on the ball. Let me explain…

Stand in such a position that your feet, hips, and shoulders are aiming just a little to the left of the target, and position your feet a little closer together than you normally would for a mid iron; do this by moving your right foot closer to your left, which will give the impression that the ball is back in your stance. Open the club face, until it aims at the target. Now swing the club along a parallel line to your feet, striking the ball with the slightly open club face, giving it clockwise spin; this will move the ball slightly from left to right. For the low one, swing the club back to your waist height and through to waist height. For the high shot, always make a full follow through.

QUICK T!P
SOFT ARMS

In a round of golf, the short iron shot is used more than you may think. The best short iron players are the ones who create the most birdie opportunities. Feel is a very important factor with this shot, the best way for you to get this feel is to address the ball and relax your arms. We call this 'soft arms'. It will not be long before you are creating the birdie chances.

Take dead aim

You know, it always amazes me when I watch a cricketer try to run one of the batsmen out, they pick up the ball, look at the wicket, and throw, very often hitting the stumps. The reason they hit the stumps so regularly is because they are trying to. This sounds obvious, and it is to them. When you are playing your approach shot from, say, 100 yards, you should take dead aim, and try to hole it. You will not hole all of them, by any means, but you will set your sights higher and consistently get the ball closer to the hole.

QUICK T!P
GET THE BALL UP TO THE PIN

If you were watching a competition from behind one of the greens, you would notice that very few players ever get their approach shot up to the hole. Try aiming to hit the top of the flag, when you are playing shots in with your short irons, this will encourage you to be a little bolder.

Let the loft do the work

The best fairway wood players are the ones who hit the ball forward, letting the loft on the club get the ball in the air. This may sound obvious, but most players go wrong by trying to help the ball in the air, resulting in hitting the ground before the ball, or in topping the shot. Commit to the shot, then let the loft do its job.

Player Profile — BOBBY JONES

Height:	5' 10"
Born:	March 17th 1902
Died	December 18th 1971
Birthplace:	Atlanta, Georgia, USA
Turned Pro:	Remained amateur

Though he played the game almost three quarters of a century ago, Bobby Jones will be forever woven into the very fabric of golf. The mere mention of his name immediately conjures up scenes that take their place among the most memorable in the history of the game: the rhythmic, perfectly balanced swing; the boyish face; the articulate, southern drawl; Augusta National; The Masters; the Grand Slam. Individually, his legacies left on the game are some of the most significant of all time. Together, they tell a wonderful story of one of the greatest the game of golf has ever seen.

Bobby Jones' accomplishments as a player are unmistakable. From 1923 to 1930, he won thirteen major championships, and remains the only player ever to win all four majors in the same year – all before retiring from competitive golf when he was just 28 years old. His playing record, alone, is the stuff of legends, but the real story of Bobby Jones is so much more. Jones was a great player, a scholar, a family man, a competitor, a writer, a teacher, a golf course designer, and, in all things, a gentleman.

Those who knew him were astounded by his talent, and touched by his humility. Indeed, one of the most fascinating and timeless stories in all of sports, is the legend of Bobby Jones.

Fairway wood ball position

The fact that you are playing the shot with a wood does not mean that you address the ball as you would a driver. All clubs, apart from the driver, should be addressed with the ball 2 to 3 inches inside the left heel, when the ball is on the ground or teed up. All clubs have a graduation of loft, from one to the next (normally 4 degrees), and, if you start moving the ball backwards and forwards in your stance, you will affect that loft.

With the correct ball position, the ball will be struck during the downswing, and the turf taken right after impact. This is necessary with all shots, apart from a driver. The ball position for a driver should be opposite the instep of the left foot. This means that, with the same swing, you will hit the ball at the bottom of the arc, or even slightly on the up swing, creating a more penetrating shot.

The only time you alter these ball positions is when you are deliberately trying to hit the ball high or low.

Control The Spin

I can almost hear you saying you would like to get some backspin, let alone control it! Club head speed and catching the ball before the ground will create plenty of backspin.

If you want the ball to stop very quickly, maybe even to spin back, use a more lofted club: you will have to create lots of club head speed to get the distance required, and the ball will stop dead. Sometimes you may not want the ball to stop so quickly, in which case, take a straighter faced club and hit the ball softer. The ball will land on the green and release up towards the hole.

Long Iron or Fairway Wood

Sometimes you play on a course only to find that you hardly used either your long irons or your fairway woods.

If you play on a course, or are going to a course, near the ocean, you can be pretty sure that the conditions are going to be completely different from those that you will find on inland courses. Normally, the courses by the ocean have firmer fairways, rather than the lush fairways found on inland courses.

The wind tends to blow harder on the coastal courses and they tend to be designed without big sand traps directly in front of the greens.

With all that said, it may be a good call to take your long irons with you instead of, say, your 5 wood when you are on the coastal course and to take your lofted fairways woods with you when playing the inland courses.

Moving the ball in the air with a fairway wood

Always remember, it is much easier to cut a ball round an obstacle, such as a tree, with a fairway wood than it is with a long or medium iron. Grip low, aim left of the obstacle, open the club face, strike the ball with an open club face, the ball will come off the club face with clockwise spin, moving the ball from left to right in the air.

Check your divot

A very quick look at the shape of your divot will tell you whether your clubs are too upright, too flat, or correct.

If you find your divot is narrow and deeper at the toe end your clubs are too flat for you, this will cause the ball to go to the right.

If the divot is narrow and deep at the heel end your clubs are too upright for you, this will cause the ball to fly left.

If the divot is the width of the sole of your club, your clubs are the correct lie for you.

Sam Snead played, tee to green, the best round of golf I have ever seen. I had just finished my first round of the Benson & Hedges tournament, at Fulford Golf Club in York. Sam Snead, who was well into his sixties, was just starting his round, so I decided to go out and watch. Every shot he played had a slight fade, from left to right. He hit every fairway and every green in regulation, apart from three par fives that he hit in two. Amazingly, he putted every green too, to score 69. If anyone else in the tournament had been putting for him, he would have broken 60.

At the end of the round, a spectator asked him how he managed to get a long iron to stop so quickly on the green. Mr. Snead asked how far the man hit his three iron, to which he replied that it was about 150 yards.

Mr. Snead's reply was, "Why the hell do you want it to stop then!" I was surprised to see that, after he had signed his card, he went straight to the practice ground to practice long shots; putting I would have understood, but long shots, the way he had just played – wow!

I plucked up enough courage to ask him why he was practicing long shots after what was the best tee to green round I had ever seen, and, as I said earlier, still is. He said that he had arrived at the course before his round and had hit some warm up shots, only to find that he was fading the ball; he decided to play the round with the fade, and now he was on the practice ground trying to find out why he was fading the ball!

You will also find a 'Player Profile' of Sam Snead on page 107.

Pitching & Chipping

" Real golfers, no matter what the provocation, never strike a caddie with the driver. The sand wedge is far more effective. "

Huxtable Pippey

Chapter 4
Pitching & Chipping

If your chip goes past the hole, do not turn away in disgust. Keep watching the line the ball rolled past on, you will then have a much better idea of the line to take when putting the ball back into the hole.

Chip under an imaginary bar

Chipping the ball properly from off the side of the green can be very rewarding, because it is a shot we are faced with time and time again. The ball should be struck in a way that makes the ball skid and then run towards the hole. The worst thing that can happen is for your left wrist to collapse through impact, resulting in a scooped shot.

1. First address the ball, holding the bottom of the grip.

2. Position the ball towards the back foot.

3. Push your knees forward, towards the target, this puts your weight onto the front foot and encourages a steep backswing, and a steep approach into the ball (essential for this shot).

4. Imagine you are chipping under an imaginary bar, this will shorten your follow through, to give the result you are looking for.

Distance control

In order to get the best out of your game, it is vital that you are able to control the distance you hit your pitch shots. If you hit your pitching wedge 100 yards, with a full swing, what do you do when you only have 75 yards to go? If you try to hit the ball more softly, you will quit on the shot and mess it up. The distance control comes from the length of your backswing. If your full backswing pitching wedge goes 100 yards, then a three-quarter length backswing, shoulder height, will carry the ball 75 yards; a backswing to your waist height, half-way back, will carry the ball 50 yards. This technique is effective with all clubs.

Perfect one distance

It is extremely difficult to become very good from 70 yards, 80 yards, 90 yards, and 100 yards, so my best advice is to become brilliant from one distance. If, at your practice range, you have a target at, say, 90 yards, keep practicing to that target until you are great at it. When you are on the course, try to leave yourself with an approach of 90 yards, whenever possible. If your ball ends up 80 yards or 100 yards away, it is much easier to play a shot by taking 10 yards off of or adding 10 yards on to the length you are brilliant at.

QUICK T!P

HIGH PITCH OR LOW PITCH?
The position of the pin will determine whether you should pitch the ball in low or high.

If the pin is at the back of the green, which would normally mean you have plenty of green to play with, a low pitch can be preferential. If the pin is at the front of the green, or tucked in behind a bunker, then a high pitch would be better.

The low pitch

The low pitch is a very useful shot. It obviously flies in low, but has plenty of backspin. Here's how to play the low pitch:

1. Position the ball back in your stance.

2. Grip the club at the bottom of the grip.

3. Put 60% of your weight on your left foot, 40% on your right.

4. Take the club back, just to waist height.

5. Accelerate through, stopping your follow through at waist height.

6. Picture the ball flying in low.

The high pitch

Here's how to play the high pitch:

1. Position the ball towards your left foot (front foot).

2. Aim your feet, knees, hips, and shoulders a little left of the target.

3. Aim the clubface at the target.

4. Swing the club along a parallel line to your feet (across the line of the shot).

5. At address, you will notice that the club head is in front of your hands. Make sure you swing the club, back, down, and through, keeping the club head in front of your hands.

6. Picture the ball flying high and make a full follow through.

The lob shot

The lob shot has been around for many, many years. It was played by opening the face of a sand wedge, increasing the loft from 56 degrees to approximately 60 degrees. In actual fact, many players still prefer to play it that way. The introduction of the lob wedge was fairly recent. This is a wedge that has 60 degrees of loft, without opening the face of the club at all. For many players, it has made the high flying pitch (lob shot) much easier to play. Whether you open the club face on a sand wedge, or use a lob wedge, there are a couple of things you should know…

1. Cock your wrists quickly on the backswing.

2. Un-cock your wrists under the ball on the downswing.

3. Keep the club head in front of your hands throughout the swing.

4. Be positive!

The ball should land softly on the green, with very little run. It is a good thought to try and slam dunk the ball straight into the hole.

DID YOU KNOW?

The most holes-in-one in a year is 28 by Scott Palmer in 1983. All were on par 3 and par 4 holes between 130 yards and 350 yards in length at Balboa Park in San Diego, California.

The most holes-in-one in a career is 68 by Harry Lee Bonner from 1967 to 1985, most of them at his 9-hole home course of Las Gallinas, San Rafael, California.

The longest hole-in-one ever recorded is the 10th (447 yards) at Miracle Hills Golf Club at Omaha, Nebraska, by Robert Mitera on October 7th 1965. A 50mph gust carried his shot over a 290-yard drop-off.

Player Profile — NANCY LOPEZ

Height:	5′ 5″
Born:	June 1st 1957
Birthplace:	Torrance, California, USA
Turned Pro:	1978

Nancy Lopez was the most celebrated player in women's golf in the decade after her rookie year, in 1978. She began playing golf as a young girl, and was an accomplished amateur before starting her professional career, while still a sophomore at Tulsa University, in Oklahoma. She won five consecutive tournaments in 1978, and everybody sort of hitched a ride on her skirt tails: the press, the fans, the sponsors, even the rest of the women playing the sport.

These were magical times for women's golf, and nobody seemed to want to get in her way. She won nine times that year, including the LPGA Championship eight times, in 1979, and she was the nicest person in the world. Lopez was named Player of the Year by the Ladies Professional Golf Association four times (1978-79, 1985 and 1988) and was inducted into the Hall of Fame when she was only 30 years old (1987). She was the youngest qualifier for the LPGA Hall of Fame, but she had to wait six months to be inducted, as the rules for admission required that a player be on tour for 10 years.

The greatest female golfer of her generation, she was also known for her cheerful persona on the course. She retired from the LPGA Tour in 2002, though she has continued to play occasional tournaments.

Bunker Play

" When I die, bury me on the golf course so my husband will visit. **"**

Joan Rivers

Chapter 5
Bunker Play

I have seen more players ruin their score by not being able to play from a bunker than from any other shot. There is a saying: A bunker shot is the easiest shot in the game. Not if you do not have a sound technique, in fact, it can be a total nightmare. The fact that we are not allowed to touch the sand with our club before we play the shot, stops us knowing the texture of the sand, or does it? When you next shuffle your feet into the sand, to get a firm footing, take a mental note. You will be able to find out how soft the sand feels, how deep the sand is, if there are any stones, or if there is any clay just beneath the surface of the sand. Knowing the conditions will help with the execution of the shot.

Backspin from the bunker

To get backspin from the green side bunker is fairly straightforward, it just needs practice.

The size of circle you draw round the ball (refer to 'The greenside splash bunker shot') determines whether the ball will stop quickly or roll. To get backspin, draw a small circle of sand around the ball, and splash that small circle onto the green. When you execute this correctly, the ball will spin plenty.

QUICK T!P

GETTING ROLL FROM THE BUNKER

Making the ball roll when it lands on the green from the bunker is again determined by the size of the circle you draw around the ball, and the amount of sand you splash out of the bunker. Draw a larger circle round the ball, splash more sand, and see that ball land on the green and roll.

Simplify the hardest shot in the game

It is widely recognized that the 50 to 60 yard bunker shot is the hardest in the game. The problem is that we are caught between it being a splash shot and long bunker shot, where we catch the ball clean. Normally, we swing far too hard at the ball, having convinced ourselves that it is a splash shot, a message is sent to our brain, during the downswing, that says we are swinging too hard at the shot, so, in a split second, we take too much sand and the ball only goes half-way. If the ball was lying in the grass outside the bunker, it would be an easy shot, wouldn't it? You would just pitch the ball onto the green.

Next time you are faced with the 50 to 60 yard bunker shot, play it the same way you would play from the grass, use a sand wedge, hit the ball, then the sand, and only hit as hard as you would from the grass. The little message will not be sent to your brain saying you are swinging too hard, and the result will surprise you.

Where a duff shot is the correct shot to play

The tip above is a great one, if the bunker has a reasonably high lip. If the bunker does not have much of a lip, and the shot is about 50 yards, try playing it this way: get your 7 iron, open the club face, NOW DELIBERATELY DUFF IT, YES DUFF IT! – take too much sand, the ball will come out low and run all the way back to the pin. THIS SHOT SHOULD REMAIN OUR SECRET.

Long bunker shot

If you have a long bunker shot, more often than not it is the result of having driven the ball into a fairway bunker. You will feel upset with yourself, and then try make up by trying to hit a miracle shot. Does that sound familiar? The first thing you must do is take a club that has enough loft to definitely get the ball out. There is no point in trying to get it out as far as possible, using a straight faced club, only for the ball to hit the lip of the bunker, and come back to where it started. Screw your feet well into the sand, for a firm footing. Imagine that the ball is sitting on a glass table top, and all you have to do is hit it clean off the top, without breaking the glass.

Bunker shot from the down slope

When playing a shot from the bunker down slope, it is natural to try to help the ball in the air; unfortunately, that is the worst thing you can do. Stand parallel to the slope, then play the shot the same way as you would play it from a flat lie. Feel like you are splashing the ball down the slope, and let the loft on the club get the elevation you need.

Bunker shot from the up slope

Normally, this is an easier shot to play than the shot from a down slope, because you have the added loft of the slope to add to the loft on your club. Remember to hit this shot firmer, because the ball will fly higher. Stand parallel to the slope, and splash the ball out in the same way as you would from a flat lie.

The pot bunker shot

You will find pot bunkers on links courses (seaside courses). These bunkers tend to be very deep, and relatively small in diameter. The only way out is with your most lofted club – a sand wedge or lob wedge.

1. Imagine the circle around the ball, as mentioned in the splash shot.

2. Stand with your feet, hips, and shoulders pointing left of the target (about 11 o'clock on a clock face).

3. Open the club face, until it points at the target.

4. Swing the club along a parallel line to your feet (across the ball).

5. Cock your wrists very quickly on the backswing.

6. The secret is to increase the loft of the club under the ball. You do this by weakening your left hand grip at address, the club will naturally open through impact.

The greenside splash bunker shot

Confidence probably plays a bigger part in the splash bunker shot than in any other shot in the game. Believe it or not, it is the ball that puts us off. We are worried that, with the speed we have to hit the sand, the ball will fly miles over the green if we catch the ball first, instead of the sand, so we take too much sand, or quit on the shot altogether.

Next time you practice your bunker shots, leave the balls outside the bunker. Draw small circles in the sand, about 5 inches across. Now practice splashing those circles of sand onto the green. It is so easy, because the ball is not there. Now go and get the balls, pop them into the bunker, and draw a similar circle around the ball. Splash that same circle of sand onto the green, the ball will ride out on the sand, and land where the sand lands. If you try not to make contact with the ball at all, only the circle of sand, this will help your confidence to such an extent, you will be telling everyone that bunker shots are the easiest shots in the game! Remember, you are not allowed to draw circles, or even touch the sand, when you are playing the course, it can only be done during practice.

A plugged lie in the bunker

We have all had them, and I am sure we have all played them badly, at some time. One great tip is to always let your opponent see the plugged

Player Profile — ANNIKA SORENSTAM

Height:	5′ 6″
Born:	October 9th 1970
Birthplace:	Stokholm, Sweden
Turned Pro:	1993

Annika Sorenstam is the best lady golfer of all time; she can compete with and beat most of the male professionals. Combining a cool efficiency with a passionate desire to win, she went on a run of success that rivals, or surpasses, anything else ever seen on the LPGA Tour, winning six times in 1997, four in 1998, twice in 1999, and five times in 2000.

Taking up golf at age 12, she quickly became good enough to start winning, and won the 1991 NCAA Championship, and the 1992 World Amateur Championship, before turning pro in 1993 and becoming Rookie of the Year on the Ladies European Tour, that year and the following. Her first win came at the 1995 U.S. Women's Open, and, from 1995 through 2006, she won eight money titles, never finishing lower than fourth, winning 69 tournaments and 10 majors in that span.

Sorenstam's domination, from 2001-2005, was complete: she was money leader, low scorer, and Player of the Year, every year. Her win totals included 11 in 2002 and 10 in 2005.

She became one of the longest hitters on the tour, without losing any of her pinpoint accuracy. Along the way, she became much more comfortable in front of the cameras, her public demeanour becoming more confident, and she won over many more fans.

ball, before you play it, then you will have a valid excuse if the ball does not come out! Like all bunker shots, the club head has to get down below the ball to have any chance of it coming out. The hard thing about playing the plugged shot is that you have to ensure that your club goes lower through the sand than normal. There are two ways of playing the plugged shot, the method you choose is determined by the height of the bunker lip.

If the lip is low, and you have plenty of green to play with, stand parallel to the line of the shot, square the club face, then drive the club down and through the sand. The ball will always roll quite a lot from this sort of lie. Experiment with both your sand wedge and your pitching wedge, to see which one works best for you.

If the lip of the bunker is high, then use your sand wedge or your lob wedge, open the clubface wide, take the club back very steeply, and then, with all your strength, bury the club under the ball. The ball should pop out.

Choosing a sand wedge

There are so many different shapes and styles of sand wedge, it can be very confusing.

There are three main things to look out for:

1. The loft should be 56 degrees for a standard sand wedge, and 60 degrees for a standard lob wedge.

2. Choose one that has a fairly rounded face, which will help when you want to open the club face, as you will not be put off by a sharp heel getting in the way and becoming too prominent.

3. Ensure your new club has plenty of bounce on the sole, to help the club splash through the sand. You can do this by resting the club on the ground and looking to see if the leading edge is off the ground, by approximately 1/8 inch.

" If you think it's hard to meet new people, try picking up the wrong golf ball. "

Jack Lemmon

I wanted to bring my friend, Gary Player, into my book, and I cannot think of a better place to introduce him than at the end of the bunker section, Gary being the best bunker player who ever lived.

I met Gary shortly after I had won the English Amateur Championship, at the ripe old age of nineteen. I had just turned professional, and was about to play my first professional tournament, the Nigerian Open. He said to me that, if I played well in Nigeria, and won enough money to get to the South African Circuit, I could stay with him and his family.

I was nineteen, and Gary was World Number One; opportunities like that do not come along very often. I won the Nigerian Open, and went to stay with Gary for four months. I did the same thing for the next seven years. I would like to say that I won the Nigerian Open each year, but I did not. Apart from my parents, and my wife Karen, Gary has been the biggest influence in my golfing career.

I remember him getting letters from the best hotels in South Africa, offering him the best suites, free of charge, during the tournaments being played in their area. They just wanted to be able to say that Gary Player was staying at their hotel. I used to travel with Gary, to these South African tournaments. He would check into the hotel while I waited outside. About five minutes later, a window would open, and Gary would shout down the number of his room. That was my cue to pick up my luggage and move in! He would order enough food for two on room service, so I used to stay in the best rooms, and eat for free, at the best hotels in South Africa. It was his idea, I might add, not mine!

Gary had a beautiful house just outside Johannesburg, in a place called Honey Dew. In the garden was a big putting green, with a variety of bunkers surrounding it. Between 6am and 8am every morning, we would practice bunker shots. He always insisted that we played for something, normally five cents for the closest, and one rand if either holed the shot. It used to cost me more than my air fare to South Africa each year! He once told me that his sand wedge was his favorite club, and that, if he had to choose between it and his wife, he would probably miss her! All very tongue in cheek, of course. My friend is definitely one of the best players to ever play this wonderful game of golf.

Putting

66 I was one under –
one under a tree,
one under a bush,
one under the water! 99

Lee Trevino

Chapter 6
Putting

No matter how good your putting stroke, if you hit the ball on the wrong line, the ball will not go into the hole. Reading the green is obviously a very important part of putting, so take your time, and notice more things about the green.

The very first thing you must do is decide how fast you would like the ball to go into the hole, do you see it dying in, or do you see it hitting the back of the hole? Having made that decision, you can start to look for slopes and grain or nap. This is the direction the grass is growing in; if you see that the grass looks dark, the grain is coming towards you, slowing down the putt, if the green gives the appearance of being light in color or shiny, the grain or nap is going away from you, speeding up the putt.

The slope can be seen from behind the ball, most of the time, but if you cannot see the slope from there, stand behind the hole and look back towards the ball. On all long putts, look from the side, to help you decide whether the putt is uphill or downhill. Having picked a line, commit to it!

Put on your shades

Sometimes it can be very difficult to read the greens; you keep coming up with the wrong line. This is very common on sunny days, so put on your sunglasses when reading the green; it makes the slope more prominent.

Be confident you have the pace of the greens

How many times do you come in from a round, only to let everyone know that you 3 putted X amount of times because you could not get the pace of the greens?

It seems that everyone has a measuring device these days, letting them know exactly how far their approach shot is, then, when on the green, they guess the distance. Next time you go out for a practice round, stop on two or three greens, pace out 15yards. Then hit some practice putts, get the feel of a 15yard Putt. During the tournament, pace out the distance of your long putts, if it's 15yards, great. If it is, say, 13 or 17yards, it is much easier to add or take away a couple of yards from a distance you are familiar with.

Reading the nap

In the UK, you do not get very much nap on the greens; (nap is when the grass grows in one direction). In some countries, the nap is stronger than the slope, which means that, if the slope of the green is from right to left and the nap is from left to right, a putt will actually go up the hill. When you are playing an approach shot, if the green looks dark, it means the nap is facing you, and the result will be the ball stopping quickly. In this instance, try to pitch the ball up to the pin. When the green looks light and shiny, the nap is growing away from you, which means the ball will land and roll, in that case, you need to pitch the ball well short of the pin and allow for the roll.

The sand wedge-putter

The mowers these days do such a wonderful job of cutting the greens, and the fringes to the greens, they quite often leave sharp edges. If your ball finishes up against one of these edges, it does not leave a straightforward shot. The most difficult one is when the ball comes against the edge, between the fringe grass, which would normally be cut to a length of ¼ inch, and the fluffy grass surrounding the fringe, which would be cut to

Player Profile — NICK FALDO

Height:	6' 3"
Born:	July 18th 1957
Birthplace:	Welwyn Garden City, England
Turned Pro:	1976

Nick is the best golfer Great Britain and Ireland has ever produced, winning six Major Championships. He had the ability to grind his opponent down, and to hit some of the finest long iron shots under pressure you would have ever seen.

In 1975, Faldo won the British Youths' and the English Amateur. The early years of his professional career were rewarding – in 1983, he won five tournaments in Europe, and had the best stroke average in the world. After winning 11 times on the European tour, and once in the United States, between 1977 and 1984, by 1985, however, Faldo had convinced himself that he wouldn't win a major championship unless he altered his swing.

In 1987, after his 30th birthday, he changed his swing, with the help of David Leadbetter, and won the Open Championship. Since then, it seems, he could hardly stop accumulating majors. In 1989, he won the Masters, and four tournaments in Europe; in 1990, he won the Masters, and the Open; in 1992, he won the Open again, and five other tournament titles.

The chief accusation is that Faldo almost made the game boring, because he has made it predictable. Certainly, at times, he seemed flawless. Certainly, he was generally the man to beat. And certainly, for Nick Faldo, a new life began at 30.

about 1 inch. You may have heard the expression, belly wedge. This is when you play the shot with your sand wedge, using a putting stroke, striking the ball on the center line. Try it the next time your ball finishes in such a position.

QUICK T!P
ON THE GREEN, PACE IS MORE IMPORTANT THAN LINE
If a caddy ever points to a line, before he has asked you how you see the ball going into the hole, do not ask him for his advice again. The first and most important thing to decide, when you are reading the green, is how you see the ball going into the hole. Do you see it dying into the hole, or hitting the back of the hole and dropping in; the line will be totally different for both. Having decided on the pace, then decide on the line.

It can still drop in!

The putt that finishes hanging over the hole is so frustrating. The fraction of an inch putt counts as much as a full drive from the tee. Next time this happens to you, try putting your shadow over the ball, sometimes the coolness of the shadow causes the grass to lie flat, making the ball topple in. Do not, however, use any other method of helping the ball into the hole!

Hover the putter

Taking the putter away smoothly is a big help. If you find this difficult, try hovering the putter about 1/8 inch above the putting surface, you will find that the putter will go back at about half the pace.

Listen – don't look!

Short putts can be a nightmare, making us frightened of them. The biggest fault I find, is when a player, anxious to see if they have holed the putt, looks up too early, the shoulders open, and the only way to get the ball in the hole is to steer it in. With any putt of four feet or below, putt the ball, and listen for the ball to drop. This will keep your shoulders square to the line. In the interest of slow play, if you have not heard anything within ten minutes, you have missed it!

Keep putting stats

It is amazing how often we blame our putting when we have a bad score. We remember the putts we missed, and forget the ones we holed. Always count and write down how many putts you had in your round – only putts from on the green. Do this over a period of 10 rounds, and see what your average is. If it is below 30, that is very good, so you can stop blaming your putting for bad scores. If it is above 33, then practice is needed. Anyone can be a good putter, it does not need strength, just practice.

QUICK T!P
USE THE MANUFACTURER'S NAME
When putting, line up the manufacturer's name on your ball with the point that you are going to hit your putt towards. Make sure you have a putter that has a directional line on it, and simply line it up with the manufacturer's line, and strike the putt.

Keep your knees still

I am sure you have heard that you should keep your body still when you are making your putting stroke. Easier said than done! A foolproof, and easy way, is to keep your knees still, which is much easier. Still knees, still body.

Let the putter head release

If you are struggling with your putting, it can often be because you have allowed your stroke to become too mechanical. For a period of time, the accepted way to putt was with a rocking motion from the shoulders, keeping the wrists firm. This can work for some, but not for all. Try letting the putter head release slightly through impact, this will give you more feel, which I believe is essential in achieving consistent pace.

Player Profile — TOM WATSON

Height:	6' 3"
Born:	September 4th 1949
Birthplace:	Kansas City, Missouri, USA
Turned Pro:	1971

By July 1975, Tom Watson was called a 'choker', a cruel label applied to this articulate Kansan, because of the manner in which he had wasted opportunities to win the US Open, in 1974 and 1975. Subsequently, nobody could have more vehemently made the point that he was a champion, rather than a chicken!

Watson won his first Open Championship that July of 1975. By 1983, he had won his fifth. Furthermore, by 1983, Watson had also won the Masters twice, and the US Open once. By 1984, Watson had taken over from Jack Nicklaus as the best golfer in the world, and he cemented that position by topping the US Money List for the fifth time, although, at St Andrews, Ballesteros denied him that coveted sixth Open. From then, his form went downhill.

But the glory days were glorious indeed. Two of Watson's triumphs will be remembered forever. His head-to-head confrontation with Nicklaus at Turnberry, for the 1977 Open, may have been the greatest major championship in history. The Young Pretender, then aged 27, prevailed with a final two rounds of 65-65 to Nicklaus's 65-66. In those days, Watson's short game was magical, and, just a month later, he won the Open Championship for a fourth time. He became only the fifth man to win both major Opens in the same year.

Move your chin to alter your backstroke

If you like to stand well away from the ball when you set up for your putt, i.e. a line from your eye to the ground would be between your feet and the ball, then your putter should travel on a slight arc (in – square – in). If your eye is above the line the ball is on, then the putter should travel straight back and straight through. If you find your putter is going back outside the line you would like, try moving your chin a little to the right, so you are looking more through your left eye, this will encourage the putter to come a little more inside on the way back. Try doing the exact opposite if your putter comes too far inside during the backswing.

Three ways to stop the yips

Players who have not experienced the yips should count themselves lucky, believe me. Having the yips is no joke. It is when your right hand decides to have a mind of its own during the impact of a putt, your mind says one thing, but your right hand takes no notice.

Most sports that require either hitting or throwing have players who will suffer this feeling. The key is to take the normal hinging of the right hand out of the stroke, by using one of the following tips:

1. Grip the putter left hand below the right, and much firmer with your left than your right. Feel as though the left hand and arm are totally in control, and that your right hand is just going along for the ride.

2. Use the claw grip. This is when your right hand grips the putter in between the middle and index finger. This will encourage a pushing motion from the right hand, rather than a releasing of the club head motion.

3. Putt left handed. Players on both the European Tour and the PGA Tour have been very successful in doing this.

" If a lot of people gripped a knife and fork the way they do a golf club, they'd starve to death. **"**

Sam Snead

You have a full set of putters in your bag!

If you are not comfortable playing a chip and run from just off the green, then putt the ball with one of your putters. In your golf bag, all of your clubs are putters with varying degrees of loft. Simply choose the putter that has got the loft to carry the ball two to three feet onto the green, with your normal putting technique, letting it run to the hole.

This method has its advantages. When did you last duff a putt?

Get a putter with loft

There are so many putters to choose from these days, it can be very confusing. It is important that you choose carefully, because they are mostly expensive, and you will use your putter for more shots than any other club. Always choose a putter that has a little bit of loft, because, when you strike the ball, your hands will be slightly in front, which de-lofts the club. Putters with no loft, therefore, have minus loft through impact, and the ball bounces as soon as it is struck.

QUICK T!P
TAKING TOO LONG OVER YOUR PUTTS?
Remaining relaxed when you are putting is very important, I am sure you will agree.

Standing over the putt for too long will make you more tense, so I would suggest that you decide on the line, address the ball, look at the hole twice, and then putt. The more times you look at the hole, the more negative thoughts you will have.

Sloping green

When you have a putt that is going to move from right to left or left to right, look at the part of the hole where the ball will enter. If you expect the ball to go into the front of the hole on sloping putts, the chances are, you will miss the putt on the low side.

Player Profile — TIGER WOODS

Height:	6' 1"
Born:	December 30th 1975
Birthplace:	Cypress, California, USA
Turned Pro:	1996

Tiger Woods is the winner of 14 of golf's major championships, and is the sport's biggest superstar since Jack Nicklaus. His father, Earl, introduced Tiger to golf at age 9 months, and, at age 2, the youngster made a now-famous appearance, putting with Bob Hope on The Mike Douglas Show.

Woods won three consecutive U.S. Amateur titles (1994-96), and, in 1996, turned pro. Woods won 46 PGA tournaments in his first ten seasons on the tour. He won the 1997 Masters in his first attempt as a pro, and later won the PGA Championship (1999), the British Open (2000), and the U.S. Open (2000), to become one of the few golfers to win all four major tournaments during their careers. In April of 2001, Woods won the Masters again, becoming the first golfer in the modern era to hold all four major tournament titles at once. In 1999-2000, Woods won six consecutive tournaments, making him the first man to do so since Ben Hogan in 1948.

Cementing his reputation as Nicklaus's heir, Woods won the British Open in 2005, the year of Nicklaus's final appearance at the competition. Although his father died in 2006, he won the British Open again that year, and the PGA Championship in both 2006 and 2007. Tiger won the US Open in 2009, with a cracked bone in his leg, totally amazing.

Accelerate the putter

Whether you are faced with a long or short putt, you must accelerate the putter through the ball. The best way to achieve this is to shorten your backswing a little, which will encourage you to accelerate through.

QUICK T!P
HIT THOSE SIX FOOT PUTTS A LITTLE FIRMER
It is quite possible to be tentative on the short putts, and lose all confidence. Try this great tip: practice by putting a ball two inches in front of the hole, then, from six feet, putt your ball hard enough to knock the other ball into the hole. This will train you to be positive, and to hit those short putts a little harder.

Green imagination

Getting the ball up to the hole on uphill putts, and stopping the ball from going too far on downhill putts, can be a problem. Next time you play golf, imagine that a hole is cut about one foot past the real hole, on uphill putts, and about one foot short of the hole, on downhill putts. Then try to hole the ball into the imaginary hole.

Difficult shots made easy with the correct club

If your ball comes to rest just off the green in a lie, such as on a bare patch where players have walked to the next tee, or in an indentation where getting the club to the bottom of the ball is impossible, or even a sandy lie that could easily cause you to duff the shot, then try putting the ball with a fairway metal. Strike the ball on the center line, and watch the ball run to the hole side. Difficult shots made easy!

Picture the ball going in

Once you have decided what line you are going to hit your putt on, make a practice stroke from opposite the ball, try to imagine that you have hit the ball and then watch that ball take the borrow and drop in the hole.

Then repeat with the actual putt, this will help with the pace of the putt and will help with your confidence, as you have already holed it once in your mind.

Hit the ball on the up swing

Keeping the ball forward in your stance and, therefore, your head slightly behind the ball at address enables you to strike the ball on the way up, this creates more top spin and a more consistent role.

DID YOU KNOW?

The world's longest golf course is the International Golf Club in Massachusetts, a long par 77, 8325-yards, from the tiger tees.

The world's highest golf course is the Tactu Golf Club in Morococha, Peru, which sits 14,335 feet above sea level at its lowest point.

The world's largest green is that of the 695-yard, par 6, 5th hole, at the International Golf Club in Massachusetts, with an area in excess of 28,000 square feet.

The world's longest hole is the par 7, 7th hole of the Sano Course at the Satsuki Golf Club in Japan. It measures a long 909 yards.

Practice Tips

" I have a tip that can take five strokes off anyone's golf game: it's called an eraser. **"**

Arnold Palmer

Chapter 7
Practice Tips

Next time you are practicing your chipping from just off the side of the green, try leaving the pin in for a couple of shots, then play the same shots with the pin out. You will find that, when the pin is out, you will be more inclined to try to hole the shot than if you leave the pin in. This is totally psychological, but it works!

Hole out before going to the tee

Confidence plays a massive part in golf; sometimes you just cannot see the ball going into the hole. Next time you play, just before you go to the first tee, go onto the putting green and putt 10 balls into the hole from 18 inches. You will get used to seeing the ball drop in, and this will give you all the confidence you need.

The shot under pressure

Let's imagine, for a minute, that you are on the last hole and that you need a par to win – drive the ball on the fairway, and hit the second shot onto the green, two putts and you're there.

Then reality comes in – a crooked drive, a chip out of the woods, miss the green with your approach, and so on. The way the Tour Professionals cope is by trying to make the smoothest, most balanced swing they have ever made. This is a great tip for those of you who get into a winning position but do not manage to pull off the win enough times.

Player Profile   SEVERIANO BALLESTEROS

Height:	6'
Born:	April 9th 1957
Birthplace:	Pedrena, Spain
Turned Pro:	1974

If Arnold Palmer had not already made golf fans aware of the word 'charisma', Severiano Ballesteros would have done it for him. He made golf as exciting to watch as Palmer did, with big hitting, a tendency to wildness, unbelievable powers of recovery, and a nerveless putting touch. Seve's unique ability to imagine and execute improbable strokes is an invaluable legacy for learning to play the game with just one club.

Ballesteros is the successor to Gary Player's position as the game's foremost international competitor, having been victorious in a dozen different national Opens, as well as winning nearly 70 times in 17 different countries. In 1979, he was the youngest winner of the Open this century, and, in 1980, he became the youngest ever winner of the Masters. By 1992, he had won at least one tournament every year for 17 seasons, a record only Player could better.

Seve was, unquestionably, Europe's leading golfer for 10 years or more, until Faldo assumed the mantle on the cusp of the 1980s and 1990s. He was the inspiration behind the European victories in the Ryder Cups matches of 1985 and 1987. It has been said that Ballesteros was born to golf, because his right arm is an inch longer than his left, making it easier for him to adopt the ideal stance.

Perfect your strike – on the beach!

Not many of us are fortunate enough to live near a beach, and even fewer of us live near a beach where you can hit a golf ball. If you are one of these lucky people, or you happen to be going on holiday to such a place, then take advantage of the opportunity. The sand must be damp and flat, and, for obvious safety reasons, you have to be well away from other people. Practice with your irons, sand wedge to long iron, and don't be happy until you can hit the ball first, then the sand. In no time at all, your entire ball striking will improve.

QUICK T!P
PUTT TO A TEE
Stick a tee into the practice putting green, and then practice putting to it. You are setting your sights higher by trying to hit the tee with the ball. Then when you go onto the course, the hole looks the size of a bucket. You can do this on the carpet at home, by turning the tee upside down.

Rehearse your first shot

Always warm up on the range before setting off on your round. Start with a lofted club, then hit some mid irons, followed by a few wood shots. You will feel warmed up and ready to go. Not quite! Now rehearse your first tee shot, with the club you intend to use from the first tee. It is amazing how much easier it makes your real first tee shot.

Look at the hole back to front

When I get to the ball on a tight driving hole, and look back to the tee, it always amazes me how easy it looks. Try it next time you play. If you are able to have a practice round on the course, make a point of looking back to the tee from the middle of the fairway, this will dispel your fears about the difficulty of some of the holes.

Fun and productive short game practice

Practicing short game can be boring, and can, therefore, be a waste of time, so here is a tip that will help make it fun and productive…

Choose four different shots to practice around the practice green, e.g. long putt, lob shot, greenside bunker shot, and a chip and run shot. Check what time you start. Start with the first shot (long putt), and stay there until you hole one, then move to the next shot (lob shot), stay until you have holed it, and so on, until you have holed all four shots. Check the time, to see how long it took you to complete. Each time you go to the practice ground, carry out the same exercise and see how long it takes. If it takes an hour at first and, within a week or two, you can do it in 3/4 hour, it shows a 25% improvement.

Breathe out to relax

Being uptight or tense when trying to hit a golf ball is fatal. Of course, it happens more when you have a difficult shot to play, or when you are doing well in a competition. When you next address the ball on the practice ground, try inhaling, and see how tense you become. Now try breathing out, and see how relaxed you become. Breathe out, hit, then inhale. This needs practice, just as much as you would practice a particular shot.

Splash the ball onto the green from fluffy lies

An easy way to drop a shot is when your ball finishes within ten yards of the green, in a fluffy lie. It's only just off the green, but sitting down low in the grass. The two shots that are card wreckers are either catching the ball too high up, resulting in the ball shooting across the green, or quitting on the shot, resulting in the ball only getting halfway.

Play the shot out of the grass in the same way you would play a bunker shot. Make sure you play it with a sand wedge, and that the clubface is well open. Be positive, and get that club under the ball. You will be surprised how often you are faced with this shot.

Warm up with two clubs

There have been a number of quite expensive warm up devices available for purchase over the years, but I still think that swinging with two clubs for a minute or two does the job best, and is certainly cheaper.

Practice chipping heights

Most of the time, we tend to practice chipping with various clubs, and rely on the loft of the club to control the height of the shot. This is all very well, and can work to a certain degree, but you can become better at those chip shots by varying the height the ball goes. First, try hitting the ball a little lower, by putting the ball back in your stance and shortening your follow through. You will notice that the ball skids and then runs. Then try putting the ball a little forward in the stance, which will make the ball fly higher. You will notice that the ball comes down with very little backspin, and, very soon, you will gain extra control.

That dreaded driving hole

Quite often, there is a hole on the course that fills you with fear from the tee. Week after week, it wrecks your card. Take five or six balls out to that tee one evening, when there is nobody about, and practice driving balls, until you start hitting the ball onto the fairway. When you arrive there during your next round, you will picture the ball landing on the fairway, and the fear of that tee shot will be a distant memory.

QUICK T!P
PRACTICE BETWEEN TWO FLAGS
A good way to be more constructive with your driving range practice, is to pick out two points on the range that are about fifteen yards apart (two flags are perfect); see how many balls in a row you can pitch between the line of the flags. This can be done with any club in your bag.

The bad first putt

If you were to hit your first putt within one foot of the hole every time, you would never three putt – well, I certainly hope you wouldn't. Again, pace is so very important.

Generally, we do not practice long putting anywhere near enough, and when we do, we put a bunch of balls down and putt them all to the same hole. When you are on the course, you only get one go at a putt, so practice that way. Put four or five balls on the putting green, and putt one ball to five different holes. Do not be satisfied until each ball is within one foot of the hole. This type of practice will eliminate your three putts.

QUICK T!P
KEEP HOLING FOUR BALLS
When you are practicing on the putting green, put four balls around the hole, at a distance of two feet. When you have holed all four in a row, put the four balls three feet away from the hole. When you have holed all four in a row, put them four feet from the hole, and so on. See what length becomes your record, and try to beat the record each time you practice, always starting from two feet.

QUICK T!P
PUTTING AT HOME
At home, put a coin down on the carpet as a point to putt from, put one ball on the carpet at that point, and another three feet away. Putt the first ball to strike the second, the second will obviously move further away. Keep taking the first ball back to the coin and putt to strike the second ball. As the second ball is getting further away, it becomes harder to hit. See how far you can get the second ball away from the coin before you miss.

Player Profile ARNOLD PALMER

Height:	5' 10"
Born:	September 10th 1929
Birthplace:	Latrobe, Pennsylvania, USA
Turned Pro:	1954

Arnold Palmer was the symbol that sold golf to the American public in the television age of the late 1950s and 1960s. He made it exciting for millions of people, by making birdies from impossible positions, and charging to victory from absolutely nowhere. Palmer attacked golf courses with brute strength, and an angelic putting touch, and he did it all with stylish flair.

His rugged good looks, magnetic personality, and ready smile, made him a hero when he won the 1960 Masters, and, two months later, the US Open. Palmer's prime years were brief, but spectacular, running from 1958 to 1964. But it was what Palmer did in those seven glorious seasons that so ignited the public interest in the man, and in his sport. He won seven majors, to add to his 1954 US Amateur title: four Masters, one US Open, and two Opens.

Palmer resurrected the fortunes of the Open Championship almost single-handedly, by persuading his compatriots to make the pilgrimage to Britain. His best golf probably came at the 1964 Masters, when he was 34. That week, Palmer was remorselessly accurate with his irons, and deadly on the greens. Nobody would have believed that it was to be his last major, but the legacy and legend of Arnold Palmer will surely be an enduring facet of professional golf.

Take your practice ground game to the course

I often get told by pupils that they hit the ball better on the range than when on the course, and they wonder how to take their game from the range to the course. There is no question that the confidence in hitting the ball on the range can be much greater than the confidence on the course. That is because it does not matter whether you hit the ball off line on the range, but it does on the course.

When you have been working on a swing change, or a particular shot, it is difficult not to revert back to your old ways when you are playing in a competition, or a match against a friend that you particularly want to win. I believe you need to take your new swing to the course in two stages. Play the course on your own first. This will give you the opportunity to try out the swing changes on the course, without being under any pressure. You will find it much easier to take the changes into competition golf, as a result.

DID YOU KNOW?

Mark Calcavecchia and John Daly were both fined by the US Tour for playing too quickly! They completed the final round in the Tournament Players' Championship in 2 hours and 3 minutes. Daly fired an 80 and Calcavecchia an 81.

" If you're caught on a golf course during a storm and are afraid of lightning, hold up a 1-iron. Not even God can hit a 1-iron. "

Lee Trevino

Making the Round Easier!

" I'll shoot my age if I have to live to be 105. **"**

Bob Hope

Chapter 8
Making the Round Easier!

If things are not going well at the start of your round, it feels good to get to the 10th tee, so you can have a fresh start.

Before you go out for your next medal round, plan what score you would be happy with for each group of 3 holes. Play the first 3 holes and bank the score, now, on the 4th, you can have a fresh start, play the next 3, bank the score, and have another fresh start on the 7th, and so on. This way, instead of waiting until the 10th for a fresh start, you can have one on the 4th, 7th, 10th, 13th & 16th.

Keep the grip light

One of the most common faults is gripping the club too tightly, especially the driver. Whenever we try to hit the ball hard, we grip hard, so hard that the knuckles go white! In actual fact, a tight grip stops you from being able to release the club head properly through impact, eliminating much of the club head speed. Grip the club as lightly as you would hold a bird, you will have more feel, less tension, and more club head speed.

QUICK T!P
DON'T JUST DRY YOUR HANDS
Most of us carry a towel on the side of the bag, to clean the ball. It is important to carry another towel to dry your hands on, when they are clammy with perspiration. Make sure the towel is wet at one end and dry at the other, so, when your hands get clammy, you can wash them and then dry them. This is much better than just drying sweaty hands.

Slippery grips can be fatal

Over a period of time, your grips will get dirty and slippery; it does not take long if your hands perspire. Slippery grips make you hold too tight, which stops you from releasing the club head through impact, resulting in a loss of distance. The best tip I can give you, for cleaning the grips and getting them tacky, is to swish the grips of each club in the dew, then let them dry naturally. The first thing to do, to hit longer shots, is get those grips clean and tacky.

When those grips get wet

I do not believe that anyone likes playing golf in the rain, especially when it is pouring down, and your grips get wet. We end up gripping so tightly, we cannot release the club head through the ball, resulting in loss of distance, or even the club! At this point, try gripping with a two-handed grip; this is when all fingers of both hands are gripping the club, with no overlapping of fingers. It will help keep hold of the club, and your right hand will release the club through impact more easily.

The ball will go with the slope

One of the most common questions I am asked, when playing a course with lots of sloping lies, is 'Which way will the ball go off a particular slope?'. When you are addressing the ball that is above your feet, the ball will fly a little left of where you are aiming. When the ball is below your feet, the ball will fly a little right of where you are aiming. An easy way to remember this is, the ball will always go in the direction of the slope.

Don't be too ambitious from the rough

There is a phrase used that I believe is worth listening to: Take your medicine.

This means that, when you have driven the ball into a bad place, do not try the shot that may only come off one in ten times. Accept the fact that you have finished in a bad position, and get the ball back in play by using the easiest shot open to you.

QUICK T!P

GREAT SHOTS INTO THE WIND

For some reason, our natural instinct tells us to hit the ball much harder into the wind. I suppose it is because we still want the ball to travel maximum distance, even though the wind is blowing into our faces. The problems start when we lose our balance, by trying to hit the ball too hard. Also, the extra club head speed created gives the ball much more backspin, which elevates the ball almost into orbit and, of course, the ball is blown off line. Try doing the opposite; hit the ball softer into the wind. You will maintain your balance, and the ball will fly on a much more penetrating trajectory. Hit the ball as hard as you like downwind.

Strengths and weaknesses

Everyone will have a strong shot and a weak shot with each part of their game, yes, including Tiger Woods! There is a gap between your strong shot and your weak shot, which you need to narrow. Let me give you an example:

Tiger prefers to hit the ball with his driver, with a slight fade, so a fade is his strong shot. He is not quite so confident hitting his drives with a draw, so a draw is his weak shot.

The gap between these shots, for Tiger, is very narrow. The gap between your favorite shaped drive and your less favorite shape may be wide. Get used to playing the golf course using your strong/favorite shaped shots, and practice your weak/less favorite shaped shots on the practice ground. You will find that you will improve your weak shots, and begin to play them on the course.

Player Profile GARY PLAYER

Height:	5' 7"
Born:	November 1st 1935
Birthplace:	Johannesburg, South Africa
Turned Pro:	1953

Gary Player lived in South Africa, but, in his heyday, you could not fly from South Africa straight to America, you had to land at London, on route. The trip could take two days. Nevertheless, in the United States, he won 21 official PGA Tour titles, and, in 1974, he became the first man to break 60 in a national championship, with a 59 in the Brazilian Open. That same season, he notched up his 100th professional title world-wide.

Player was the third link in golf's 'Big Three' – Palmer, Player & Nicklaus. He won the first of his three Opens in 1959, the first of his three Masters in 1961, the first of two PGAs in 1962, and his one US Open in 1965.

Gary Player is still acknowledged as the master bunker player, and he never gives up. On the way to winning one of his five World Matchplay Championships, in 1965, he beat Tony Lema after being 7 down with 17 holes to play and, in 1978, he won his third Masters title, aged 42, by shooting a 64 on the last day, to snatch victory. Even today, he believes he could win a major championship. Player owes much to his unquenchable spirit. His strict adherence to a fitness regimen throughout his career has meant he is still in enviable condition.

Take an energy drink out on the course with you

There are very few sports that take as long from start to finish as golf. Keeping your concentration and energy levels up during the second half of the round is difficult, causing you to hit tired shots and perhaps losing your match.

The Tour Professionals have realized that having an energy drink as they start the back nine holes helps them maintain their energy and concentration levels. The most popular, by far, is a can of Red Bull. Do as the professionals do, you will be happy with the results.

Clean grooves for more control

One of the biggest differences between Tour Professionals and the weekend golfer, is the way the professionals look after their clubs. They religiously keep the grooves on the iron faces clean and free from clogging. Many amateurs I teach allow the grooves on their irons to fill up with dirt, so the ball is then unable to grip the face of the club. The result? No backspin.

Be one step ahead

Nowadays, whether you are planning a golfing trip away from these shores, or intending to visit a different part of the country to play some golf, it is important to book your golf in advance. My tip is to use the internet for your golf bookings. You can check out the type of courses, the cost for a green fee, and surrounding attractions and facilities. Booking online gives you peace of mind, and you can quite often benefit from discounted rates. Have fun planning your next golfing trip!

QUICK T!P
RAIN-SOAKED GLASSES

If you wear glasses when you play golf, you are at a definite disadvantage when it starts to rain. The spots of rain get onto the lenses, and you can see a number of golf balls. Wearing a cap, or visor with a big peak, is a help, but wiping the lenses with a cloth can smear them, making your vision even worse. I have found that a small piece of chamois leather wiped onto the lenses is great, and can be used very quickly and effectively.

Shiny shoes

Do you know, I have never seen a great player with dirty shoes? To play your best, you have got to feel and look the part. Can you imagine going for an interview, for a very important job, with mud on your shoes? Chances are, you would not perform to the best of your ability. If you get a great shine on your shoes, you will look and feel good. Remember, confidence is a big part of the game.

Keep your head warm

There cannot be many worse feelings than being on a golf course, miles from the clubhouse, when it's bitterly cold. If your hands are cold, you cannot grip the club properly, if your body is cold, you cannot turn properly. Put on a woollen bobble hat, you will find that your body stays much warmer. Think of how cold your house would be if there was no insulation in the roof, it works the same way.

Arrive in plenty of time

It is very important to find out what is a suitable amount of time you need to allow for travelling from the airport, or your hotel, to the golf course. Some people like to arrive at the course an hour before teeing off. This gives about a 1/2 hour to hit the ball and a 1/4 hour to get in some putting. Other players like to arrive only 3/4 hour before the start of their game. Many amateurs, I have seen, tend to arrive with so little time to spare, they end up tying their shoe laces on the way to the first tee! Then they wonder why they get off to a bad start!

66 Golf is like chasing a quinine pill around a cow pasture. **99**

Winston Churchill

BE PREPARED FOR ANYTHING
The obvious things to remember are your clubs, your golf balls, your tees, your score card, a pencil, a pitch fork, etc. The not so obvious things can also be very important, but easy to forget. Make sure you always keep a small first aid kit in your bag: things such as plasters, in case of blisters, headache pills and insect repellent, can prevent you from having a miserable time out on the course.

The worst weather I ever had to play in

One year, I was playing in the John Player Classic at Turnberry, Scotland, and the forecast was terrible for the whole week. There was a pro-am the day before the tournament, and the worst of the weather took place on that day. I finished my round, having been buffeted all over the place, and went to the dry and warmth of the changing rooms. The first person I saw was a British comedian called Kenny Lynch, and I asked how he had got on. He told me he had been playing with Douglas Bader, a war hero who had lost both his legs. He was now walking and playing golf, with the aid of artificial legs. Kenny went on to tell me that they had only played two holes, when Douglas said, "Come on Kenny, got to go in, my legs are full". When he got inside, they had taken off Douglas's legs and poured out the water. And we think we have troubles!

Use the rules to your advantage

Knowing the rules can help you; here are a few that you need to know:

LOCAL RULES

Knowing all, or even most of the rules, of golf is just about impossible, and the key is to know where to look up the rule in the book. Local rules are always on the back of the score card, and on the notice board at the golf club; make sure you read these rules, because they over-rule the rules of golf. A great example is stones in bunkers. In the rule book, you will notice that you are not allowed to remove stones in bunkers, but, quite often, the local rule for the course allows the removal of stones in bunkers. So, if a stone is impeding your shot, it pays to know the rule!

WHEN IS THE BALL IN A HAZARD?

A hazard will be marked by a red or yellow line, depending on whether it is a water hazard or a lateral water hazard. Your golf ball is deemed to be in the hazard when the ball touches a part of the line, unlike an out-of-bounds white line, where the entire ball has to be over the line.

CASUAL WATER

Did you know that your ball is regarded as being in casual water when it is lying in surface water, on or off the fairway? It is also in casual water when you are able to squelch up water, whilst taking your stance. The rule says that you can drop the ball within one club length from the closest point of relief. This means that, if your ball is in casual water in the rough, and the closest point of relief is on the fairway, you are allowed to drop on the fairway.

OUT OF BOUNDS

For your ball to be out of bounds, and to incur a two-shot penalty, the entire ball has to be over the out of bounds margin.

DROP THE BALL CORRECTLY

During your round, you may have to drop your ball, either as a free drop or under penalty. This is how you drop correctly:

If you are entitled to a free drop, you will be able to drop the ball within one club length of the closest point of relief. You can use any club to measure that one club length, it does not have to be the club you intend to play the shot with. Measure the distance by laying the club down on the ground, and then putting a tee in the ground at the one club length distance. Now, stand facing the target, from waist height, and with an arm outstretched arm from the side of your body, drop the ball within the club length. If the ball happens to roll outside the club length, that is fine, providing it does not come to rest either nearer the hole, or more than another two club lengths outside the tee you put down as a measurement, in which case, you have to drop again. If your drop is under penalty, and the rule says you have to drop within two club lengths, exactly the same procedure applies, except that the measurement is two club lengths instead of one.

RABBIT SCRAPE UNDER A BUSH

This can be an awkward one. If your ball is in a rabbit scrape under a bush, it may not give you the free drop you were expecting. You only get a free drop if you can see a way of playing the shot, though not if it is impossible to hit the ball – in this case, you would have to drop the ball under a penalty of one shot. If your opponent asks for a free drop from a rabbit scrape under a bush, ask whether they would have tried to play the shot from there, if the ball was not in the scrape. If they say no, do not give them a free drop.

QUICK T!P
THE IMPORTANCE OF THE SHORT GAME

Teaching juniors is the most enjoyable part of my career; they have so much natural ability. Over the years, I have taught hundreds and hundreds of boys, through the English Golf Union Coaching Programme. I watch the top juniors in the country hit golf balls as well as a ball can be hit, then I ask them the question, "How many of you want to turn professional?" All put their hands up. My reply is that, if any of you end up with a good short game, you will live in a caravan for the rest of your life. Any of you who end up with a great short game, will live in a mansion. Sometimes the message sinks in as easily as the ball!

Player Profile — SAM SNEAD

Height:	5' 11"
Born:	May 27th 1912
Died	May 23rd 2002
Birthplace:	Ashwood, Virginia, USA
Turned Pro:	1934

Samuel Jackson Snead who was one of the top players in the world for most of 4 decades, and he left an indelible mark on the game. He won a record 82 PGA Tour events, and about 70 others worldwide. He won seven majors: three Masters, three PGA Championships, and one British Open, but he failed to win a U.S. Open. However, it is unfair to dwell on the one blemish in a career that features a record 84 official US tour victories.

Snead liked to cultivate his rustic image as the hillbilly boy from mountain country, and he was famed for his folksy image, wearing a straw hat, and playing tournaments barefoot. He has also been admired by many for having the most natural, fluid, so-called 'perfect swing', and generated many imitators. The physical ease with which he could generate immense power enabled him to become the first golfer to break 60 in a significant competition; to be the oldest winner of a US tournament (52 years 10 months); to finish third when aged 62 in the 1974 US PGA Championship, and to be the first man to beat his age on the US tour (scoring 66 when he was 67). Like Ben Hogan, Snead suffered terrible putting problems (the 'yips') as his career progressed, leading to him trying several different techniques on the greens.

My Favorite Courses

Some of my Favorite Golf Courses

I tend to like all golf courses, but some more than others. I prefer courses that test your skill, rather than the ones that give the advantage to the really long hitters. There are so many courses that have shallow fairway bunkers, even if your ball goes in, you can get out with a long iron, or even a wood. This type of course allows you to blast the ball from the tee, without worrying about the bunkers. I much prefer bunkers to be proper hazards, if you go in one, you need a sand wedge to get out. As you can imagine, the courses I like most, are links courses.

Here are some courses I love; if you get the chance to play any of them, treat yourself!

Course	Country	Page Index
Gary Player Country Club	South Africa	112
Saunton	England	113
Machrie	Scotland	114
Blue Canyon	Thailand	115
Royal St George's	England	116
Royal Birkdale	England	117
St Andrews Old Course	Scotland	118
Kingsbarnes	Scotland	119
San Lorenzo	Portugal	120
Loch Lomond	Scotland	122
Hunstanton	England	123
Blairgowrie	Scotland	124
Royal Porthcawl	Wales	125
Malone	Ireland	126
Grayhawk	USA	127
Champions	USA	128
Dunes West	USA	129

❝ Golf, like the measles, should be caught young, for, if postponed to riper years, the results may be serious. **❞**

P G Wodehouse

Gary Player Country Club
Location: Sun City, North-Western South Africa

The Gary Player Country Club is acknowledged as a difficult and demanding course. Since 1981, it has been home to the Nedbank Million Dollar Golf Challenge. The course requires stamina and accuracy from players. The comparatively flat nature of the golf course is misleading – water hazards, cunningly sited bunkers, and pins hidden away on kidney shaped greens make up for the lack of gradient.

Off the back markers, the course measures over 7000 meters, which makes it one of the longest in the world. But a variety of tees make it possible to shorten the course, and render it playable for all levels of golfer. A distinguishing feature of the course is its green's complexes, with strategically placed bunkers, swells, and mounds that protect the super, slick, clover shaped greens. With pristine, perfect kikuyu fairways, and excellent bent grass greens, the course is in perfect condition all year round.

A feature hole? Well, they're all good, but, for risk and reward, the stand-out is the 9th. Play this par 5 from the forward tees, and then have a go for the island green with your second, and get the thrill of the challenge of this superb test of golf.

Course details:

Founded:	1979
Designer:	Gary Player
Length:	7,587 Yards (championship)
	7,147 Yards (club)
Par:	72
Grass Type:	Fairways – Kikuyu
	Greens – bents

Saunton – East Course

Location: Saunton, Near Braunton, Devon, England

Right from the first tee, your experience on the East Course, running through the majestic dunes of Braunton Burrows, is inspirational. The opening hole, playing from an elevated tee to a valley-like fairway, is a truly superb hole, and it requires two fine strokes to find the target. Other holes of note on the front nine include the par four, 3rd, where the green has an uncanny knack of dismissing all but the most perfect of shots; and the short 5th, which, though measuring just over 120 yards, can cause considerable anguish, with its dramatically sloping green.

The homeward trip provides no less a test. From the notoriously hard-to-hit par three, 13th hole, the finish is tough, to say the least. The immense 455-yard par four, 14th, requires something special to achieve par, while the tee shot on the par five, 15th, is over the dunes to an angled fairway. It's probably the 434-yard 16th, however, that is the most spoken about hole on the East Course at Saunton. Boasting a fairway that curves to the left, and skirts the sides of the dunes, an array of ridges, and a bunker complicates the approach to the green.

Course details:

Founded:	1897
Designer:	Herbert Fowler
Length:	6,729 Yards
Par:	71
SSS (course rating):	73
Course Type:	Links

Machrie

Location: Port Ellen, Isle of Islay, Scotland

There are many reasons why you have to come and play the Machrie, one of Scotland's oldest and most traditional links, not least of which is to discover why so many golfers find it a bewitching and exalting experience. It is now getting a wider name for itself as one of the world's top links courses.

This course, laid out in 1891 by Willie Campbell, hosted its very own Open Championship in 1901, when a trio, by the names of Harry Vardon, John Taylor and James Braid, competed for a £100 first prize, reputed to be the largest prize of its kind at that time in the British Isles.

The main feature is the number of blind holes, and blind shots, that have to be negotiated from undulating, tight fairways onto wonderful, rolling greens. The views of the bay are another aspect that has made the Machrie the favorite it is today. At 6,324 yards long, we like to think of the Machrie course as a subtle beast with a sense of humor. In the natural sand dunes lurk its wicked teeth, and a capricious temperament sometimes provoked by winds of varied strengths and direction.

Course details:

Founded:	1891
Designer:	Willie Campbell
Length:	6,324 Yards
Par:	71
SSS (course rating):	70
Course Type:	Links

Blue Canyon

Location: Phuket, Thailand

Canyon Course

This championship course has featured in many major golf tournaments, and, with the use of existing canyons and rubber plantations, was designed with minimal disruption to the natural landscape. The Canyon has an intriguing mix of narrow, tree-lined fairways, requiring accurate tee shots. A number of dog legs demand precise shot making, and there is a selection of testing Par 3's. These features, along with numerous water hazards, long carries, and the beautifully manicured fairways, all lend themselves to one of Asia's most sought after golfing destinations.

Lakes Course

The Lakes offers a whole new challenge to the game of golf, with water hazards on 17 out of 18 holes. It is a mixture of water-filled canyons, created by open cast mining, with its natural land flow left relatively unchanged. It was designed to cater for a broader range of golfers. A total of five sets of tees offer a complete golfing experience. Its front 9 holes run through a landscape of lakes and natural canyons, whilst the back 9 weaves its way through scenic lakes and soft, whispering rubber tree woodlands. Gentle winds, at 10mph, constantly add a challenging dimension to any game.

Course details:

Founded:	Canyon – 1991, Lakes – 1999
Designer:	Yoshikazo Kato
Length:	7,179 Yards (Canyon), 7,129 Yards (Lakes)
Par:	72
Grass Type:	Fairways – Zosyia Matrelia
	Greens – Bermuda Tiff Dwarf

Royal St George's

Location: Sandwich, Kent, England

Royal St. George's (also known affectionately as Sandwich) is one of the great links courses of British golf. The layout at Sandwich has changed little, and the fact that the course is rated so highly to this day is a testament to the fine initial design. It has played host to many famous Opens through the years, and is one of the toughest courses of the lot, particularly for the higher handicap golfer. The carries required to find fairways, which tumble amidst towering dunes, are almost all long, while some of them are also blind.

Each hole at Sandwich offers a stiff challenge, and real muscle is almost always required on the par fours. For the ordinary player, the huge 4th either incites a laugh or a cry. With two sleeper-lined bunkers awaiting the drive, and a wickedly elevated green, access in two strokes is practically unthinkable. Three of the four closing holes are long, two-shot par fours, with the closing hole measuring almost 470 yards, requiring two majestic strikes.

The test may be fierce, and the fairways can be extremely fast when it's sunny, but, no matter how difficult, Royal St. George's has an appeal like no other.

Course details:

Founded:	1887
Designer:	Dr. Laidlaw Purves
Length:	6,930 Yards (championship)
	6,607 Yards (club)
Par:	70
SSS (course rating):	74
Course Type:	Links

Royal Birkdale

Location: Birkdale, Southport, Merseyside, England

Though a relative newcomer to the Open Championship rota, only hosting its first Open in 1954, Royal Birkdale is regarded by many as the finest championship venue of them all.

It is an exceptionally fair course, and, if you hit the fairways, rarely will the ball be thrown off course. The fairways are laid out in the flat-bottomed valleys between the towering dunes, but Royal Birkdale is a very tough cookie to master. The greens were re-built prior to the 1998 Open and, despite their youth, are extremely difficult to read.

It is impossible to select any particular hole for special praise on this great course. Suffice it to say that, right from the off, having negotiated a 450-yard par four, double dogleg start, Royal Birkdale will provide the links purist with a profound golfing experience.

Royal Birkdale can be a torrid experience when the wind is up, with white horses kicking and rearing their heads in the Irish Sea, crashing like kamikazes onto the beach. But, whatever the weather, Royal Birkdale is a provocative place to play golf, one that will linger in your memory as long as you live.

Course details:

Founded:	1889
Designer:	J. H. Taylor, F. Hawtree, M. Hawtree
Length:	7,300 Yards (championship)
	6,690 Yards (club)
Par:	72
SSS (course rating):	73
Course Type:	Links

St Andrews – Old Course

Location: St Andrews, Fife, Scotland

The Old Course is the cultural and historical home of golf, with the game being played here since the 15th Century. It has evolved over time, and, despite its reputation and status, it is a public course. It is also unusual in that it starts and finishes in the town.

It is known for its particularly physical features, including 112 bunkers, some of which are especially famous, e.g. 'Hell' on the long 14th, 'Strath' on the short 11th, and the 'Road Bunker' at what is probably the most famous golf hole in the world, the 17th or 'Road Hole'.

The oldest golf course in the world has many remarkable features that help make it so special to golfers around the world, including the double greens, where the outward and inward holes are cut on the same putting surface. These greens are large, not surprisingly, and golfers can be faced with putts of almost 100 yards.

From the moment you arrive at the first, you cannot help but be absorbed by a sense of occasion, anxiety and, ultimately, excitement. This sense of exhilaration never dissipates, as you stride along fairways so often trodden by golfing greats, past and present.

Course details:

Founded:	1400
Designer:	Various incl. Daw Anderson (1850s); Old Tom Morris (1860s – 1900); Dr. Alister Mackenzie (1930s)
Length:	6,566 Yards (championship)
Par:	72
Course Type:	Links

Kingsbarns

Location: Kingsbarns, Fife, Scotland

Directly on the North Sea coast, only six miles from St. Andrews, Kingsbarns is, without a doubt, one of the most breathtaking links courses ever developed. Though it only opened for general play in July 2000, the links appears to have been in situ for centuries, as golf was played on this very site as far back as 1793.

Kingsbarns Golf Links is a real one of a kind, in that it is a new, man-made development. With views of the ocean, and the high tide foaming over the rocks below, this links is special, and is infinitely more scenic. It is a worthy spiritual descendant of its historical neighbor, the Old Course.

The sea figures prominently on every hole, with the sights, sounds and smell of the ocean spray. The links boasts spacious fairways, which roll and twist through majestic dune ridges and hollows. While its large, inviting greens present the golfer with subtle challenges. Combined with true links turf, and associated contours, Kingsbarns Golf Links is distinctly playable, but challenging to the end.

Remember the name Kingsbarns Links, as you will be hearing so much more about this course in the years to come.

Course details:

Founded:	2000
Designer:	Kyle Phillips, Mark Parsinen
Length:	7,150 Yards (championship)
	6,754 Yards (club)
Par:	72
SSS (course rating):	73
Course Type:	Links

San Lorenzo

Location: San Lorenzo, Algarve, Portugal

Located in the Quinta do Lago estate, and forming part of the Natural Park of Ria Formosa, San Lorenzo enjoys a reputation for being one of the best golf courses in Europe. The hotel and golf club are unique when it comes to outstanding views, a calm and tranquil setting, and for showing nature at its best.

The course features large, fast greens and undulating fairways, which meander through avenues of pine trees. There are some spectacular holes overlooking the sea, which also border lakes abundant with wildlife. A round on this course begins with an enticing, but almost unachievable, Par 5, before continuing to the three following holes along rolling, pine tree-fringed fairways. It is from the 5th, however, that the most extraordinary part begins, offering wonderful views over the Atlantic Ocean. At the 8th, the course turns back inland and faces the largest of the lakes. For the next four holes, the course turns seawards again, and ends with the daunting 18th. This is a tricky par-4, mainly involving a lake and a semi-island green waiting for the inaccurate shot, but is, nevertheless, one of the best finishing holes in golf.

Course details:

Founded:	1988
Designer:	Joseph Lee
Length:	6,822 Yards
Par:	72
Course Type:	Links

❝ Don't play too much golf. Two rounds a day are plenty. ❞

Harry Vardon

Loch Lomond
Location: Luss by Alexandria, Dunbartonshire, Scotland

Tom Weiskopf created one of the world's greatest courses along the bonnie, bonnie banks of Loch Lomond. Framed by towering hills, and bounded by the loch, the course, with its lush fairways and large, beautifully manicured greens, winds through an abundance of trees and wild life, without seeming to disturb a blade of grass.

It also reeks of exclusivity. And exclusive it is. The closest many can come to appreciating its style is by watching it on TV. Only a member can invite you to play, and even the members are not encouraged to over-golf!

It starts gently enough, to put you at your ease, and soon you are marvelling at the difference of each hole. To pick out a favorite is difficult, but there's the 6th, the longest hole in Scottish golf, at 625-yards. It runs majestically alongside the loch, and it's not a step too long. The 14th sorts out the men from the boys. Go for the green over the bog or bale, out to the fairway on the left. If you're lucky enough to play here, you won't be trying to recount the memorable holes, you'll be struggling to forget any one of the 18.

Course details:

Founded:	1994
Designer:	Tom Weiskopf & Jay Morrish
Length:	7,095 Yards
Par:	70
Course Type:	Links

Hunstanton

Location: Old Hunstanton, Norfolk, England

Though not quite as tough as some of the Open Championship courses, Hunstanton is still a real challenge for all links enthusiasts, being of the highest calibre, and offering countless, superb holes and greens that are amongst the finest and slickest in England.

Following the opening couple of holes, one encounters what is rated as the toughest hole on the course. The key to this long, well-bunkered, right hand dogleg 3rd is good positional play. The short par four, 6th hole, demands a knee-trembling second, to a green set high on a plateau, while the 168-yard, 7th, requires a carry over a wild ravine and steep bunker.

Like the opening half, the homeward journey does not disappoint, with one of the finest holes being the par four, 13th. Aim straight for the marker post on the distant ridge, as anything right will be lost or in rough, and anything left will probably find a large, steep bunker. The long par three, 14th, requires a blind shot aimed at a distant pole, and, though this is the kind of hole that would never be built today, it is full of character and bares testament to the history of the course.

Course details:

Founded:	1891
Designer:	James Braid, James Sherlock
Length:	6,911 Yards
Par:	72
SSS (course rating):	72
Course Type:	Links

Blairgowrie

Location: Rosemount, Blairgowrie, Perthshire, Scotland

The Rosemount course, at Blairgowrie Golf Club, situated at the feet of the Grampian Mountains, is a beautiful heathland golf course, lined with forest of pine and silver birch, and is one of the most admired in this area. There is a liberal sprinkling of heather, broom, and gorse off the fairways, which, at the right time of year, add considerable color to a lovely setting shared with the exquisite wildlife, including deer, red squirrels, woodpeckers and oyster catchers, to name but a few.

The crisp turf has a moorland feel to it, with the fairways pitching and rolling through avenues of trees. Each hole is carved through the trees, which provide a natural amphitheater for a calm and tranquil round of golf. From start to finish, the holes are good and varied, but the best holes are left until last. The 17th is especially noteworthy, a lovely par three called "Plateau", with a two-tiered green. There is nothing dramatic or significantly difficult about this layout. You can open your shoulders, as the fairways are generously wide. The course is maintained to a very high standard, and all this makes for a good, honest and enjoyable round of golf.

Course details:

Founded:	1889
Designer:	James Braid
Length:	6,590 Yards
Par:	72
SSS (course rating):	73
Course Type:	Heathland

Royal Porthcawl

Location: Porthcawl, Glamorgan, Wales

One of the finest links courses in the world, Royal Porthcawl is renowned for the quality of its greens, and boasts a magnificent setting, offering views of the sea from every hole.

The first three holes skirt along the beach, and often play directly into the prevailing wind. Shots on the 2nd and 3rd holes are particularly tricky, and can easily be destined for a sandy lie on the beach, which is, of course, out-of-bounds. The par five, 5th hole, is an interesting one in that it, somewhat unusually, climbs steeply to the green, while the relatively short 9th hole has a wickedly sloping green, guarded by a number of bunkers.

The homeward journey will not disappoint. The 440-yard par four, 13th hole, invites a downhill drive from the tee, into the wind, and a well-hit second to the green. Running in opposite directions, the 15th and 16th, both par fours, total over 900 yards between them. Aptly, the closing hole is a memorable one, where you are faced with an approach to a green running from front to back, requiring careful putting. The player is continuously tested by varying wind speed and direction, and will almost certainly need to use every club in their bag.

Course details:

Founded:	1891
Designer:	Tom Simpson
Length:	6,691 Yards (championship)
Par:	72
SSS (course rating):	74
Course Type:	Links

Malone

Location: Belfast, County Antrim, Northern Ireland

Malone is one of Ireland's best parkland golf courses, and it is virtually unknown. This Championship course is set in 300 acres of secluded wooded parkland, in gently undulating countryside, just 5 miles from Belfast city center, in the lower Lagan Valley at Ballydrain.

The front nine is called Drumbridge, and the back nine is called Ballydrain – named after the local area. Malone is a solid test of golf. Accuracy from the tee is demanded, because many mature trees await to stymie the wayward tee-shot. Malone offers a good deal of interest and variety – there are many memorable holes. None more so than Malone's signature hole – the charming short Par 3, 15th – where the tee-shot must be played across a gorgeous, 27 acre lake. It's amazing what such an expanse of water can do to the nerves! The same lake comes into play on the 18th, where the drive must carry the corner of the lake. It's a cracking end to a lovely, parkland golf course.

If you are in Belfast, and you've got your clubs handy, make sure you play Malone. You'll be hard pressed to find a better parkland course in Northern Ireland.

Course details:

Founded:	1962 (present site)
Designer:	J. Harris (C K Cotton Associates)
Length:	6,600 Yards (championship)
Par:	71
SSS (course rating):	72
Course Type:	Parkland

Grayhawk

Location: Scottsdale, Arizona, USA

Since opening in 1994, Grayhawk Golf Club has become one of Arizona's most celebrated, daily-fee golf clubs, mostly because of Grayhawk's two exceptional 18-hole golf courses – Talon and Raptor. Both have earned numerous awards and accolades over the years, and have hosted high-profile competitive events, such as the PGA Tour's Frys.com Open (2007 – 2009). Other PGA Tour-sanctioned events include the Andersen Consulting World Match Play Championship (now known as the Accenture Match Play Championship), Tommy Bahama Challenge, the Williams World Challenge (now known as the Target World Challenge), FBR Open Pro-Ams, Tommy Bahama's Desert Marlin, Thunderbird International Junior, and The Detour.

The course provides breathtaking views of the near by McDowell Mountains, as well as the distant skyline of Phoenix.

There is a premium for positioning your tee shot on the correct sections of the desert style fairways.

This truly is one of the most beautiful places to be on a golf course.

Course details:

Founded:	1994
Designer:	David Graham
Length:	6973 Yards (championship)
Par:	72
SSS (course rating):	73
Course Type:	Desert

Champions

Location: Houston, Texas, USA

Champions Golf Club was founded by Jack Burke, Jr. and the late Jimmy Demaret, in 1957. From its origin, Champions has consistently carved its place in golf history, hosting such prestigious events as the Ryder Cup Matches in 1967, the United States Open in 1969, and the Champions International, a PGA tour event.

The Cypress Creek Course was designed by Ralph Plummer, and opened for play in 1959. With over 70,000 trees, wide fairways, and enormous greens, it remains one of America's premier tournament sites.

When you play this magnificent course, you cannot help but realize that you are playing from turf all the great champions have been on before.

The clubhouse is unbelievable, with changing rooms bigger and better than most peoples' houses.

When I played the course, I was fortunate to meet Jack Burke, a legend in the game of golf, I will never forget it.

Course details:

Founded:	1957
Designer:	Plummer & Fazio
Length:	7120 Yards (championship)
Par:	72
SSS (course rating):	73
Course Type:	Inland/Tree-lined

Dunes West

Location: Charleston, Mount Pleasant, South Carolina, USA

Located on the site of the historic Lexington Plantation is Charleston's nationally acclaimed golf facility, Dunes West Golf Club. This Arthur Hills design is a diamond. This par 72, 6,871 yard masterpiece is one of the best you will ever play. Set amid Bermuda-covered dunes, and 200 year old oaks draped in Spanish moss, this course blends its historically rich environment with the best golf facilities offered anywhere today.

The Dunes West clubhouse, which was built on the site of the antebellum Lexington Plantation, was specifically designed to capture the old, southern charm of the Low country. This tremendous course takes full advantage of its fabulous setting.

Dunes West Golf & River Club is truly a world-class golf experience. And remember, it's not whether you win or lose, but where you play the game that counts.

A great challenge and you will want to return as soon as possible.

Course details:

Founded:	1950s
Designer:	Arthur Hills
Length:	6871 Yards (championship)
Par:	72
SSS (course rating):	73
Course Type:	Dunes

"My swing is so bad I look like a caveman killing his lunch."

Lee Trevino

Glossary

Glossary of Golfing Terms

Ace	A hole-in-one, made in one stroke.
Address	The stance taken by a player preparing to hit the ball. The positioning of the body in relation to the golf ball. (Same as "addressing the ball").
Aggregate	A score made over more than one round of play, or by two or more players partnering each other.
Air shot	When a player intends to play a shot, but misses the ball completely.
Albatross	A score of 3 less than par for that hole, e.g. 2 shots on a par 5.
Alternate ball	Format in which players alternate hitting each other's ball on each stroke, until the hole is finished. For example, after teeing off, player one hits player two's ball, and vice versa.
Amateur	A golfer who plays without monetary compensation.
Angle of approach	The angle or degree at which the club moves downward, or upward, towards the ball.
Approach shot	Normally a short or medium shot played to the putting green or pin.
Apron	The grassy area surrounding the putting surface. (See 'Fringe').
Attack	To play aggressively, and with purpose.

Attend the flag	To hold and then remove the flag while another player putts.
Back door	The rear of the hole.
Back lip	The edge of the bunker that is farthest from the green.
Back nine	The last 9 holes of an 18 hole course.
Backspin	A reverse spin placed on the ball, to make it stop short on the putting surface.
Backswing	The backward part of the swing, starting from the ground and going back over the head.
Ball at rest	The ball has come to a complete stop on the fairway or green.
Ball marker	A token or a small coin used to spot the ball's position on the green prior to lifting it.
Banana ball	A slice that curves to the right, in the shape of a banana. An extreme slice.
Best ball	A match in which one player plays against the better of two balls, or the best ball of three players. Also applies to the better score of two partners in a four-ball or best-ball match.
Better ball	A match play or stroke play game where two players on a side each play their own ball, with each team choosing the better of their two scores.

Birdie	A score of 1 less than par for a hole, e.g. 3 shots on a par 4. Possibly derived from the term "It flew like a bird", to indicate a good shot.
Bird's nest	A lie in which the ball is cupped in deep grass.
Bite	The backspin imparted on the ball that makes the ball stop dead, or almost so, with little or no roll.
Blind hole	If the putting green cannot be seen by the player as he approaches, the hole is called blind.
Bogey	A score of 1 more than par for that hole, e.g. 4 shots on a par 3.
Borrow	To play to one side of the hole, to compensate for the slope of the green.
Break	The way in which the ball will roll or bounce. Also the sideways slope on the green.
British Open	"The Open" – the first one ever held. The National Championship put on by the Royal and Ancient Golf Club of St. Andrews, Scotland.
Bump and run	A chip shot, including the run of the ball after landing. Also known as 'chip and run'.
Bunker	A depression in bare ground that is usually covered with sand. Also called a "sand trap". It is considered a hazard under the Rules of Golf.
Buried ball	A ball partially buried beneath the sand in a bunker.
Carry	The length of travel by the ball after it is struck, to the place where it first hits the ground.

Casual water   Any temporary accumulations of water visible before or after a player takes his stance, but is not a hazard or in a water hazard. A player may lift his ball from casual water without penalty.

Chip shot   A short approach shot of low trajectory, usually hit from near the green. It is normally hit with over spin or bite.

Chip and run   A chip shot, including the run of the ball after landing. Also known as 'bump and run'.

Chip in   A holed chip shot.

Chop   To hit the ball with a hacking motion.

Claggy   As in "I've got a bit of a claggy lie". A lie that is a bit wet and muddy – of British origin – almost a claim for casual water, but not quite!

Claim   The term used in match play to denote a protest by a player, regarding a possible breach of the rules.

Closed stance   The left foot extends over the ball's line of flight, while the right foot is back.

Closed face   The clubface is pointed to the left of the target when you address the ball.

Cock   To bend the wrists backwards in the backswing.

Collar   The grassy fringe surrounding the putting green.

Condor   A 4 under par shot; e.g. a hole-in-one on a par 5. Has occurred on a hole with a heavy dogleg, hard ground, and no trees. Might also be called "a triple eagle".

Cross-bunker	A lengthy bunker that is situated across the fairway.
Cross-handed grip	A grip where the left hand is below the right.
Cup	The container in the hole that holds the flagstick in place.
Cut	The score that reduces the field to a pre-determined number, and eliminates players in a tournament. Usually made after hole 36 of a 72 hole tournament.
Cut shot	A controlled shot that results in the ball stopping almost immediately on the green, without roll.
Divot	A piece of turf removed by the club when making a shot. It is always replaced and tamped down.
Dogleg	A left or right bend in the fairway.
Dormy	When playing in match play, it is an expression used when you are as many holes up as there are left to play, so you cannot lose, e.g. 3 holes up with only 3 holes left to play. (Sometimes spelled 'dormie').
Double bogey	A score of 2 more than par for that hole, e.g. 6 shots on a par 4.
Double eagle	A score of three under par for a single hole. (Same as "Albatross").
Down	Being a specific number of holes behind your opponent.
Downhill lie	When addressing the ball and your right foot is higher than your left (for right-handed players).
Downswing	The motion of swinging a club from the top of the swing to the point of impact.

Draw shot	A controlled "hook" used to get in position for the next shot, or to get out of trouble. To play a shot so that it curves, owing to sidespin, from right to left for a right-handed player, or from left to right for a left-handed player.
Drive	To hit the ball with maximum force and full stroke, usually with a driver from the tee.
Driver	The farthest-hitting modern wooden club, used primarily from the tee, when maximum distance is required. Also called the No. 1 wood.
Driving iron	Another name for the No. 1 iron. Formerly one of various iron clubs used for shots through the green.
Drop	To deposit the ball on the course in order to put it back in play, after it has been declared unplayable or after the ball has been lost.
Eagle	A score of 2 less than par for that hole, e.g. 3 shots on a par 5.
Face	The hitting area or surface of the club head.
Fade	A term used to describe the slight turning of the ball from left to right (by a right-handed player) at the end of its flight. From right to left for a left-handed player.
Fairway	The area of the course between the tee and the green that is well-maintained, to allow a good lie for the ball.
Fairway wood	Any wooden club other than a driver.

Flier	A ball is hit without spin, and goes a greater distance than normal.
Fluffy lie	A ball that is sitting up in grass.
Follow through	The continuation of the swing after the ball has been hit.
Fore	A warning shouted out to advise anyone who may be in danger from the flight of the ball. The problem is that nobody knows who is being shouted at, so everyone ducks.
Four ball	A match in which the better ball of two players is played against the better ball of their opponents.
Foursome	A term given to four players playing together. Also a match in which two players play against another two players, with each side playing one ball.
Free drop	A drop where no penalty stroke is incurred.
Fried-egg	A ball half-buried in the sand.
Fringe	The area surrounding the putting green, which is sometimes cut to a height lower than the fairway, but not as short as the green itself. (Same as "Apron").
Gimme	Short for 'Give Me'. It is a term used when your opponent has one putt left that you don't think they will miss. You say "That's a gimme" and concede the putt. Only permitted in match play.
Grain	The direction in which the grass on a putting green lies, after it has been cut short.
Grand Slam	The four major championships: the British Open, the U.S. Open, PGA Championship, and the Masters.

Graphite
A lightweight material used to make shafts and clubheads.

Green
According to golf rules, the whole golf course. However, in popular usage, it refers to the putting surface.

Green fee
The charge made (by the club) to allow the player to use the course.

Green jacket
The prize awarded to the winner of the Masters Tournament.

Hack
To chop violently at the ball. To make bad shots. To play bad golf.

Hacker
An unskilled golfer.

Half
Used in match play, when score is tied on a hole. Each side is credited with a half.

Half Shot
A shot played with less than full swing.

Halved
When a match is played without a decision. A hole is "halved" when both sides play it in the same number of strokes.

Handicap
The number of strokes a player may deduct from his actual score, to adjust his scoring ability to the level of a scratch golfer. Golfers are given a handicap according to their ability, and the better player then gives shots to the poorer player. It is designed to allow golfers of different abilities to compete on the same level. Golf is the only game in the world where a good player can play a poor player, and they can still have a very good, close game.

Hanging lie	A ball resting on a downhill slope.
Hold	To hit the ground and stay in place, with little roll or bounce.
Hole high	A ball that is even with the hole, but off to one side.
Hole in one	A hole made with one stroke. (Same as "Ace").
Hole out	To complete the play for one hole by hitting the ball into the cup.
Honour	The privilege of hitting first from the tee. Usually assigned at the first tee. After the first tee, the privilege goes to the winner of the previous hole.
Hook	When a ball spins in such a way that it moves in the air from right to left, for a right-handed player, and left to right, for a left-handed player.
Impact	The moment when the ball strikes the club.
In	The second 9 holes, as opposed to 'out' – the first 9 holes.
Interlocking grip	A type of grip where the little finger of the left hand is intertwined with the index finger of the right hand, for a right-handed player. The converse applies to a left hander.
Intended line	The line you expect the ball to travel after being hit.
Iron	Any one of a number of clubs with a head made of iron or steel.
Kick	Another term for bounce. Usually an unpredictable or erratic bounce.

Lay up   To play a shorter shot than might normally be attempted. Would be used to achieve a good lie short of a hazard, rather than trying to hit the green in one less shot.

Lie   The position where the ball rests on the ground. The lie can be good or bad, in terms of the nature of ground where it rests, the slope, and the level of difficulty in playing it. Can refer to the number of strokes played during the hole.

Line   The ideal path of a putt to the hole. Also, when on the fairway, the correct direction the ball is to be played toward the green.

Links   Originally meaning a seaside course, it is now used to mean any golf course.

Lip   The top rim of the hole or cup.

Lob shot   A shot that goes straight up and comes almost straight down, with very little spin or forward momentum. Useful when there is not much green to play to.

Local rules   A set of rules for a club, determined by the members.

Loft   The elevation of the ball in the air. Also means the angle at which the club face is set from the vertical, and is used to lift the ball into the air. It is measured precisely as the angle between the face and a line parallel to the shaft.

Long game   Shots hit with the woods and long irons.

Long irons	The relatively straight faced, and longer hitting irons.
Make the cut	To qualify for the final rounds of a tournament by scoring well enough in the beginning rounds.
Marker	A small object, like a coin, that is used to mark the spot of the ball when it is lifted off the putting green.
Match play	A competition played where each hole is a separate contest. The team or player winning the most holes, rather than having the lowest score, is the winner. The winner of the first hole is "one up"; even if the player wins that hole by two or three strokes, he is still only "one up". The lead is increased every time the player wins another hole. The winner is the player who wins the most holes. This was the original form of golf competition.
Mid-iron	An iron club with more loft than a driving iron. Another name for a 2 or 3 iron.
Misread	To putt wrongly. Not to read the green correctly.
Municipal course	A public course owned by a local authority.
Nineteenth hole	The bar at the clubhouse.
One up	Used in match play, meaning to have scored one hole more than your opponent. Also, the score of the player who is one up.
One-putt	To hole the ball using only one shot on the green.
One-wood	Alternative name given to the driver.
Open	A tournament where both amateurs and professionals are allowed to play.

Open stance	The left foot is dropped behind the imaginary line of the direction of the ball. This allows the golfer to turn more in the direction the ball is going to travel.
Out	The first 9 holes of an 18 hole course. The second 9 holes are "in".
Out of bounds	The area outside the course where play is prohibited. A player is penalized on stroke and distance, i.e. he must replay the shot with a penalty of one stroke.
Overlapping grip	As used by a right-handed player, having the little finger of the right hand overlapping the space between the forefinger and second finger of the left hand. The opposite for a left-handed player.
Par	The number of strokes a player should take to complete a round with good performance. Par for each hole is normally determined by the length of the hole. Generally, a hole shorter than 245 yards is a Par 3; between 245 yards and 475 yards, a Par 4; longer than 475 yards, a Par 5. Level Par for 18 holes is the equivalent of having parred every hole.
Peg	A tee.
Penalty stroke	An additional stroke added to a player's score for a rules violation.
Pick up	To take up one's ball before holing out. In match play, this concedes the hole, or, in stroke play, incurs disqualification.
Pin	Same as "Flagstick".

Pin-high	A ball even with the pin, but off to one side. (Same as "Hole high").
Pin placement (pin position)	The position of a hole on a putting green on any given day.
Pinehurst	A variation of play where one partner plays the other's drive. One ball is then selected to finish the hole.
Pitch	A short shot, lofting the ball into the air in a high arc, and landing with backspin.
Pitch and putt	A short golf course designed primarily for approaching and putting.
Pitch and run	The same as a pitch shot, but hit with a lower-numbered club to reduce loft and backspin. This allows the ball to run after it lands on the putting green.
Pitching irons	The short irons.
Pitching wedge	An iron club designed for making pitch shots.
Play off	To determine a winner in a tied match by playing further holes, or a further round.
Playing professional	A professional golfer who primarily competes in tournaments.
Playing through	Passing another group of players who are playing ahead.
Preferred lie	Local rules that allow a player to improve his lie in a specific manner without penalty.

Pro-Am	A competition that pairs professional players with amateurs.
Pull	A ball that goes to the left of the target with little curve, as hit by a right-handed player. The converse applies to left-handed players.
Punch	Low, controlled shot into the wind. It is made by slamming the club down into the ball with a short swing.
Push	A ball that goes to the right of the target, with very little or no curving for a right-handed player. The converse applies for a left-handed player. (As opposed to "Pull".)
Putt	The shot made on the putting green. From a Scottish term meaning 'to push gently or nudge'.
Putt out	To hole the ball with a putt.
R & A	Royal and Ancient Golf Club of St. Andrews.
Reading the green	Determining the path the ball will take on its way to the hole, by analyzing the contour and texture of the green.
Release	The point in the downswing where you uncock your wrists.
Reverse overlap	For a right-handed player, a putting grip where the index finger of the right hand overlaps the little finger of the left; the converse applies for a left-handed player.
Rim	To run round the edge of the cup.

Road hole	The 17th hole at St. Andrews. Reputed to be the most difficult hole in the world.
Rough	Long grass areas adjacent to the fairway, greens, tee off areas, or hazards.
Rub of the green	Any accident, not caused by a player or caddie, that moves or stops a ball in play, and for which no relief is given under the rules. This is when your ball is deflected by agencies beyond your control that are not part of the match, or the competitor's side in stroke play. A bit of bad luck.
Run	The distance the ball rolls on the ground, or when it lands on the ground.
Run-up	An approach shot that is close to the ground, or on the ground.
Sand iron	Also called a sand wedge. A heavy, lofted club that was used for playing from bunkers. It is no longer in use.
Sand Trap	A depression in bare ground covered in sand, also called a bunker. Considered a hazard under the rules of golf.
Sand wedge	An iron with a heavy flange on the bottom, primarily used to get out of sand traps.
Scratch	Par play. A zero handicap.
Scratch player	A player who has no handicap.
Shank	When the ball is struck at a point on the golf club where the shaft joins the head (the shank of the club), resulting in the ball flying off in a direction about 45 degrees to the intended line.

Short game	The part of the game that is made up of chip shots, pitching, and putting.
Short irons	The highly lofted irons.
Slice	What happens when a ball spins in such a way that it moves in the air, from left to right for a right-handed player and right to left for a left-handed player.
Stroke play	A competition where the total number of strokes for one round, or a pre-determined number of rounds, decides the winner.
Stymie	When an opponent's ball is in the line of the other player's putt. Since the ball may now be lifted, the term is used, these days, to refer to a tree or object in the way of a shot.
Sudden death	In a match or stroke competition, when the score is tied after completing the round, play continues until one player wins a hole.
Sweet spot	The dead center of the face of the club.
Takeaway	The start of the backswing.
Tap in	A very short putt.
Tee	A disposable device, normally a wooden peg, on which the ball is placed, for driving. Also refers to the area from where the ball is hit on the first shot of the hole. Originally a pile of sand used to elevate the ball for driving.
Tee off	To play a tee shot.

Tee up	To begin play by placing the ball on the tee.
Tee-shot	A shot played from a tee.
Texas wedge	What the putter is called when it is used from off the green. Also a shot played with a putter from outside the putting green.
Topspin	The forward rotation of the ball in motion.
Touch shot	A very delicately hit shot.
Triple bogey	This term is used when a golfer is 3 over par on a hole.
Turn	To start the back 9 holes.
Un-cock	To straighten the wrists in the downswing.
Under clubbing	Using a club that does not give the needed distance.
Unplayable lie	A lie where the ball is impossible to play, such as in a thicket of trees.
Up and down	Getting out of trouble, or out of a hazard, and into the hole.
Water hole	A hole with water, such as a stream or lake, which forces the players to shoot over it.
Wedge	An iron with a high loft, used for short shots, e.g. pitching wedge, sand wedge.
Win or lose by, say, 4 & 3	This is when you are more holes up than there are left to play, so you have won, e.g. 4 holes up with only 3 holes left, so you win 4 & 3.

Wood   A club, either wood or metal, that has a large head and is used for shots requiring greater distance. Usually a numbered set of 5 or more, starting with the driver and proceeding to the 5 wood.

Yips   Shakiness or nervousness in making a shot. You cannot make your hands do what you want them to do, and they seem to have a mind of their own. Normally, the yips happen on the putting green, and, instead of a nice smooth stroke at the ball, you get a very jerky action.

Has Technology Helped the Game – It's Debatable!

During the early years of golf, the club shaft was made of hickory, the club head was either wood or metal, and the grip was leather. The ball was made of feathers, packed into a leather skin. Wow, how things have changed!

I believe that much of the skill has been taken out of the game by the fact that the ball is now made in such a way that it is difficult to slice or hook it; in short, the ball has been designed to go straight, and to go a long way. The club heads are made of materials like titanium, the shafts are graphite, and the grips of materials that help you hold on in all kinds of weather conditions.

It is amazing to see the distance some of the best players hit the ball; most of the time, they are left with short iron shots to the green. The need for long irons is gradually disappearing, in fact, many players, professional and amateur, are using a club called a rescue club, instead of a 1, 2 or 3 iron. The rescue club can only be described as a cross between an iron and metal wood.

The number one wood (driver) has become approximately twice the size of the old wooden headed club, and is now made from titanium. The idea is to get a larger sweet spot from which to strike the ball; this will ensure that a miss hit is not as destructive as it would have been with the old club.

Technology is taking golf equipment to new levels, as it has done in most other sports. Unfortunately, the distance the ball now travels has made thousands of golf courses a little short, with bunkers out of position to catch the stray shot, and so on.

The rules say that we are permitted to carry a set of fourteen clubs; I believe that the skill factor would remain if we were only allowed seven, meaning that golfers would have to make up more shots than they do at present. The manufacturers would then be encouraged to design a golf ball that can be moved in the air easier, bringing skill back into the game, rather than distance.

Having said all that, I am sure that the best players would still be the best players.

DID YOU KNOW?

Fourteen clubs are the maximum allowed in one player's bag. Any number below 14 is fine, but more than 14 is not. Also, those 14 clubs cannot be changed during the course of one round. You must finish with the 14 you started with. (There are some exceptions in the case of a club breaking.)

However, if you begin with fewer than 14, you may add clubs during a round as long as no delay is caused and as long as the club or clubs added are not borrowed from another player.

The penalty for exceeding the 14-club rule in match play is a loss of hole for each hole played in violation of the rule, up to two holes lost. In stroke play the penalty is two strokes for each hole played in violation of the rules, with a maximum of four strokes.

The Golf Ball – Now and Then

Three basic types of golf ball have figured in the development of the game – the feathery, the gutta percha, and the now familiar rubber-cored ball.

The feathery that was used virtually unchallenged for almost 400 years until the mid-19th century. This ball consisted of a spherical outer shell which was stuffed with a large quantity of feathers that had been boiled to soften them and make them more compact. The hole through which the feathers were rammed was sewn up, and the ball was then hammered into a sphere. The resultant ball was rarely spherical and so would fly erratically and roll unreliably. On wet days it would soak up water, making it inconsistent in weight and so difficult to play. The water would also rot the stitching, causing the ball to split open on stony ground.

When, around 1850, the properties of a Malaysian gum called gutta percha were discovered. This could be softened in hot water, rolled into a sphere and then hardened by cooling. The result was a perfect sphere that rolled true for the first time in the history of the game – the 'gutty'. These balls were cheap and quick to make and, although not as pleasant to hit as the feathery, were clearly an improvement. They occasionally shattered, but could be remolded. There was initially, however, a problem. The smooth balls would not fly any distance. Eventually it was noticed that if a ball was dented during play, it then flew better. Thus the gutty users began hammering dents into their balls – inadvertently establishing the principle of the modern dimpled ball. The gutty now flew perfectly and became the standard ball for the next 50 years.

At the turn of the century, a man named Coburn Haskell introduced the soft-cored elastic wound ball. Initially wrapped in gutta percha, this ball was livelier and more resilient. It was regarded with suspicion, and the authorities seriously discussed banning it. This changed, however, during a practice round at the 1902 British Open between the professional

Alexander Herd and the gifted amateur John Ball. Herd should have won easily, but found himself consistently outplayed. Ball was using one of the new balls. Herd was invited to try one and remarkably went on to win the championship. The ball became an overnight success.

Since then, the rubber-cored ball has become the standard for all golfers. Despite wrangles over the weight and size that began after World War I, a decision was finally reached in 1968 that in any PGA competition worldwide only the American standard of 1.68 inches diameter would be admissible.

Modern technology continues to play its part in the development of the golf ball, making it increasingly more consistent both in flight and roll. Other refinements have included polymer coatings and the introduction of solid and semi-solid balls. Also the pattern and number of dimples has been changed together with variations in the compression to suit individual players and playing conditions.

My List of the Greatest Golfers of all Time

(Not necessarily in order!)

Player	Page Index
Gary Player	100

I think the most sensible way of choosing a list of the greatest golfers of all time, is by looking at their record. Gary lived in South Africa, but, to prove himself as a champion, he had to win in the USA and Europe. When Gary was in his heyday, you could not fly from South Africa straight to America, you had to land at London, on route. The trip could take two days. Gary went on to win nine Majors, the Grand Slam, five World Matchplay championships, and numerous events throughout the world.

| **Jack Nicklaus** | 14 |

Jack simply has the best record, eighteen Majors. It is very possible that will never be beaten.

| **Bryon Nelson** | 30 |

Bryon Nelson won eleven tournaments in a row on the PGA Tour. Totally amazing.

Player	Page Index
Sam Snead	107

I did watch Sam play once. It was, and still is, the finest tee to green round of golf I have ever seen. He was a true athlete, and won more professional golf tournaments than anyone else.

| **Bobby Jones** | 41 |

Bobby Jones always remained an amateur, but he still won the world's major championships; he had a swing to die for.

| **Annika Sorenstam** | 61 |

Annika is the best lady golfer of all time; she can compete with and beat most of the male professionals.

| **Nancy Lopez** | 53 |

A great champion, she kick-started the ladies game.

Player	Page Index
## Ben Hogan	24

I was never fortunate enough to watch Ben Hogan, but all those who did, say he was the greatest ball striker of all time. There is, and always will be, a certain mystique about Ben Hogan.

Lee Trevino 23

One of the finest ball strikers of all time, he could just about make the ball talk, which was something else he was good at.

Nick Faldo 71

Nick is the best golfer Great Britain and Ireland has ever produced, winning six Major Championships. He had the ability to grind his opponent down, and to hit some of the finest long iron shots under pressure that I can remember seeing.

Tom Watson 74

Anyone who can win The Open five times has got to be on my list of all time greats. Tom has a swing that will last and last.

Player	Page Index
Tiger Woods	79

In the year 2001, everyone, myself including, thought it was just a matter of time until Tiger overtook Jack Nicklaus in the number of Majors won. Tiger is still winning Majors, albeit a little slower than a few years ago. If anyone can overtake Jack Nicklaus, it will be Tiger.

Severiano Ballesteros	86

Lee Trevino once said that Severiano Ballesteros plays shots none of us thought possible. Seve is the most exciting player I have ever seen, and he brought European golf to life in the late 1970s, right the way through to the present day.

Arnold Palmer	91

Arnold became famous for his charge to the front of the leader board. Along with Jack Nicklaus and Gary Player, he was known as one of the Big Three. Arnold has done as much as, if not more than, any other player to develop Professional Golf throughout the world.

Index